The Unitarian Universalist Pocket Guide

Edited by
William F. Schulz

Second Edition
Skinner House Books
Boston

Printed in the United States of America.

99 98 97 96 95 94
10 9 8 7 6 5 4 3 2

Cover design by Suzanne Morgan

The Unitarian Universalist pocket guide. — 2nd ed. / edited by
William F. Schulz.
p. cm.
Includes bibliographical references.
ISBN 1-55896-319-7
1. Unitarian Universalist churches—Handbooks, manuals, etc.
I. Schulz, William F. II. Unitarian Universalist Association.
BX9841.2.U55 1993
289.1'32—dc20 93-22694
CIP

Contents

Unitarian Universalist Principles

We, the member congregations of the Unitarian Universalist Association, covenant to affirm and promote:

The inherent worth and dignity of every person;
Justice, equity, and compassion in human relations;
Acceptance of one another and encouragement to spiritual growth in our congregations;
A free and responsible search for truth and meaning;
The right of conscience and the use of the democratic process within our congregations and in society at large;
The goal of world community with peace, liberty, and justice for all;
Respect for the interdependent web of all existence of which we are a part.

—*from the By-Laws of the Unitarian Universalist Association*

Preface

For almost forty years, the Unitarian Universalist Association (UUA) has introduced itself to prospective members by means of the *Pocket Guide*. For all of those years (including the period before 1961, when a predecessor organization called the American Unitarian Association published it), the *Pocket Guide* was edited by the Rev. Harry Scholefield, one of our most distinguished and beloved ministers. With this revised edition Harry has retired from the editorship. But his spirit lingers, and it is to him that this volume is dedicated.

Most of the essays that follow are new. Only Harry's own, "Our Roots," remains from the last edition. And even that has been expanded—to more adequately honor our Universalist heritage—with the help of Paul Sawyer, minister of the Berkeley, CA, Fellowship of Unitarian Universalists.

That past essays should be replaced with new ones in no way means that they were inadequate. It only suggests that ours is a dynamic faith and that the details of our institutional life change rapidly.

Beth Graham's essay, "Our Ministry," offers a good example of that. The community ministry of which she speaks did not even exist as a formally recognized category of ministerial fellowship when the last *Pocket Guide* appeared. Beth, who is associate minister of the First Parish in Concord, MA, describes that form of ministry as well as others in which all of us, lay and ordained, share.

The fourth through sixth essays offer a taste of three critical aspects of life in our congregations and our larger movement. Mark Belletini, minister of Starr King Unitarian Church in Hayward, CA, and recently retired chair of a commission charged with creating a new Unitarian Universalist hymnbook, describes worship in a Unitarian Universalist setting. Makanah Morriss, Director of the UUA's Department of Religious Education, offers a sense of how we educate our children, youth, and adults in the truths and mysteries of religion. And Judith E. Meyer, minister of the Unitarian Community Church of Santa Monica, CA, describes how we apply our religious principles in the world.

"Our Commitment to Racial and Cultural Diversity" is not only a new essay but a new topic for the *Pocket Guide.* It reflects our renewed devotion to making Unitarian Universalism a truly diverse and inclusive religious community. Melvin A. Hoover is Director of Racial and Cultural Diversity at the Association.

In the back of the *Pocket Guide* you'll find information about the Unitarian Universalist Association and the Church of the Larger Fellowship (CLF). Also included are important dates in our history, a bibliography, and resources for additional information. Many thanks to former UUA Director of Information Mark Harris, now minister of the First Parish Unitarian in Milton, MA, for his assistance with these sections.

Obviously this little book can only whet your appetite for finding out more about us. To experience Unitarian Universalism in full flourish, you need to participate in one of our congregations. To learn of the congregation nearest you, feel free to call the UUA at (617) 742-2100 or write us at 25 Beacon Street, Boston, MA 02108-2800.

I've been privileged to serve as President of the Association since 1985 and am about to retire from the post. I've enjoyed helping put this edition of the *Pocket Guide* together, including the first essay, which attempts to introduce you briefly to our beliefs and tradition.

Those of us whose words appear within these pages can only hope that you find our religion as meaningful to you as it is to us. We don't believe that Unitarian Universalism can "save" you in the traditional sense—or even that everyone in the world ought to be Unitarian Universalist (little danger though there be of that!). But we do believe that, if you are looking for a community within which you and your children can explore the common questions of humanity without fear or guilt, we may well have something to offer. And we do believe that the world would be a far happier place if more people took our faith and values as their own.

Join us, won't you? We're eager to meet you.

William F. Schulz
UUA President, 1985-1993
January, 1993

Our Faith

Andrei Sakharov, the renowned Russian physicist, once asked his wife, Elena Bonner, "Do you know what I love most of all in life?" "I expected," Bonner confided some years later to a friend, "that he would say something about a poem or a sonata or even about me. But no. Instead, he said, 'The thing I love most in life is radio background emanation'"—the barely discernible radio waves which reach us here on earth from outer space and reflect unknown cosmic processes that ended billions of years ago.

What Sakharov meant of course was that he loved the mysteries which the cosmos hands us, the grandeur and immensity of this thing we call Creation. And he loved the fact that we human beings can occasionally get a glimpse of those mysteries and that grandeur, even the parts whose work was done billions of years ago.

Very few of us can ask the kind of sophisticated questions of the universe which an Andrei Sakharov did. Even fewer have the opportunity to receive a hint of a reply. But most of us at one time or another wonder about the ultimate questions of life: How did Time begin? Is there a God? Has life meaning? What is good? Why must we die?

These are fundamental religious questions. And most religions—at least in their orthodox varieties—believe they have the answers. Those orthodox answers may be framed in terms of Jesus Christ (Christianity), the law of the Covenant (Judaism), or the eight-fold path to Enlightenment (Buddhism), to name but three.

Unitarian Universalism is different. We respect the answers offered by Christianity, Judaism, Buddhism, and the world's other great faith traditions—we even draw our inspiration and some of our forms of worship from those traditions—but *we respect the mystery more.* We believe, in other words, that no single religion (or academic discipline, for that matter) has a monopoly on wisdom; that the answers to the great religious questions change from generation to generation; and that the ultimate truth about God and Creation, death, meaning, and the human spirit cannot be captured in a narrow statement of faith. The mystery itself is always greater than its name.

This, then, is why ours is a *creedless* faith and respect for others' beliefs is a high value. We do not require our members to subscribe to a particular theology or set of affirmations in order to join our congregations. Instead, we encourage individuals to garner insights from all the world's great faiths, as well as from Shakespeare and from science, from feminism and from feelings. We invite people to explore their spirituality in a responsible way. We ask Unitarian Universalists to cherish the earth, to free the oppressed, and to be grateful for life's blessings. Out of this combination of reflection and experience, each one of us shapes a personal faith. For Unitarian Universalists the individual is the ultimate source of religious authority.

Tradition and Community

But while the individual is the ultimate source of religious authority, the individual is not the *only* source. If that were the case, Unitarian Universalists could easily fall prey to the condition that afflicted Otto von Bismarck, of whom it has been said that "he believed firmly and deeply in a God who had the remarkable faculty of always agreeing with him." No, our individual predilections need to be tempered by conversation with our tradition and tested within the crucible of our community.

Our history is important to us. Both our Unitarian and our Universalist traditions rejected the notion that "higher" authorities—be they theologians or bishops, rabbis or preachers—could impose their views upon the laity. This is the historical source of our commitment to freedom of belief, congregational polity, and lay empowerment. But our traditions also supply us with a rich legacy of positive affirmations, from Universalism's faith in the benevolence of God to Unitarianism's assurance that human beings have within them the capacity to shape the future.

The result is that today our tradition provides us with a lodestar and a sort of "early warning system" for the recognition of tenets at odds with the norms of our faith. The tradition is not definitive—it will inevitably be modified and even superseded by new "revelation"—but if you hear someone preaching hellfire and damnation or that the future is solely in the hands of God, chances are it's not a Unitarian Universalist!

And the other resource which helps shape our faith is the religious community. When I was in Hong Kong not long ago, I saw a sign in the window of a dentist's office which read, "Teeth extracted by the latest Methodists." To my knowledge, teeth extraction is not (yet) one of the things our congregations provide their members, but a supportive context within which to pursue one's religious pilgrimage certainly is. If what we discover on that pilgrimage is ever to realize its full potential, it must be shared, pondered, and tested with others.

Individual freedom of belief exists, then, in dynamic tension with the insights of our history and the wisdom of our communities. It is this tension which puts the lie to the oft-heard shibboleth that Unitarian Universalists can believe anything they like. It is true that we set up no formal religious test for legal membership, that we welcome the devout atheist as readily as the ardent Christian, but it is *not* true that one can subscribe to views at variance with our most basic values. Clearly, one could never advocate racism or genocide, for example, and still in any meaningful sense call oneself a Unitarian Universalist.

Commitments and Covenants

Though we have no creed, we surely have made covenants—with each other, with previous generations, and some would even say with God—to live as a community united around certain precepts. The most recent form of those commitments we hold in common are to be found in our Principles and Purposes. But what of those most fundamental religious questions to which I referred earlier? What does Unitarian Universalism have to teach us about God and meaning, the Good and suffering?

Obviously our answers may differ in detail depending upon our theological perspectives. Some of us would understand God in very personal ways, as the source of love or hopefulness; some would see God in nature or as Ultimate Reality; others would take the Goddess as a model; and still others would have no truck with the whole notion at all. Similarly, some of us would find life's greatest meaning through Christian prayer or Buddhist meditation; others through communion with the natural world or the pursuit of scientific understanding; and still others through the companionship of their loved ones. It is this very diversity which makes Unitarian Universalism a congenial home for those who come from different religious backgrounds.

Regardless of the details or differences, however, there are a whole host of faith affirmations with which the vast majority of us would be comfortable. Let me offer a selection. This is of course my own way of putting it, but it would, I think, be recognizable to most of my co-religionists:

- *Whatever we think the holy be, Creation itself is holy.* We make no distinctions between the natural and supernatural, the secular and sacred. We simply cherish the earth and all its creatures, the stars in all their glory.

- *Life's gifts are available to everyone, not just the Chosen or the Saved.* Only human artifice or blind ill fortune can separate us from the source of blessings. Whatever that source be, it makes no artificial distinctions among its supplicants.

- *That which is Divine (or, if you prefer, most precious and profound) is made evident, not in the miraculous or otherworldly, but in the simple and the everyday.* We look not to the heavens or an afterlife for our meaning, but to the exuberance of life's unfolding. Whatever abundance there may be is lodged right here on earth.

- *Human beings themselves are responsible for the planet and its future.* Social justice is a religious obligation. The future is never fated.

- *Every one of us is held in Creation's hand—we share its burdens and its radiance—and hence strangers need not be enemies.* The "interdependent web of all existence" offers an embrace to everything and everyone. Our only inherent enemies are violence, poverty, injustice, and oppression. The earth is our cherished home.

- *Though death confronts us all, we love life all the more even though we lose it.* An honorable and impassioned life may not deny death its due, but it can surely rob it of victory.

A Wide and Generous Faith

I am a third-generation Unitarian [Universalist]. This religion runs in my blood. It has spurred me and soothed me. But most Unitarian Universalists are at one time or another newcomers to our faith. Ninety percent of us come out of other religious traditions; some come from none at all. This makes for both richness and confusion.

Nonetheless, regardless of background, we each share a few fundamental convictions. Finally, let me put it this way. Too often in this world, religion has been the agent of division and fear. Unitarian Universalism seeks to heal a fractured world and the broken lives within it by calling every one of us to the best that is in us. Beyond nationalism and ethnic prejudice, beyond materialism and greed, beyond the petty and the shallow—we invoke a global loyalty, an ecological ethic, and a deeper mercy.

In the last analysis our Unitarian Universalist mission and the faith which sustains it is clear and straightforward: *we would treat the wounds of a narrow spirit with the salve of a generous heart.* How better than that to eradicate fear? How better than that to honor life's mysteries?

William F. Schulz

Our Roots

The Unitarian Universalist Association is of recent origin. It came into being in Boston, MA, in 1961, with the merger of the American Unitarian Association and the Universalist Church of America. But the Unitarians and Universalists each have their own distinct histories. So it is that the Association and the more than 1,000 churches and fellowships which form its constituency have roots that run to the distant past.

Origins of Our Faith

The term Universalism has taken on different meanings at different times. There is an important element of truth in this comment by Universalist minister L.B. Fisher: "Universalists are often asked to tell where they stand. The only true answer to give to this question is that we do not stand at all, we move." In 1791, the Universalist Benjamin Rush, a physician and a signer of the Declaration of Independence, described Universalism as "a belief in God's universal love to all His creatures." He went on to say that God "will finally restore all of them who are miserable to happiness."

Taken by itself, this was a remarkable statement in an age when belief in eternal hellfire and damnation was common. But Rush went further and declared that the belief in God's universal love "leads to truths upon all subjects, more especially upon the subject of government. It establishes the *equality* of mankind [sic]—it abolishes the punishment of death for any crime and converts jails into houses of repentance and reformation." The fact that the early American Universalists saw social action growing inevitably out of theological belief should not be lost on us.

Scholars trace Universalism all the way back to the Alexandrian Christian School and the early church fathers, Clement of Alexandria and Origen in the third century. Some would claim that the roots go back even farther—to the universal inclusiveness of Jesus' gospel message or in the teachings of the Buddha and Confucius. The Universalist belief that the whole human race will be "saved" was condemned as a heresy by a church council in 544.

Unitarianism is similarly ancient and heretical. Unitarian origins actually can be traced to the early Greek faith in the unity of all existence and to the belief of early Jewish Christians in the human prophet Jesus as the Messiah, or Son of Man, ushering in the new reign of God. The first official use of the term, however, occurred in 1638 in Transylvania, a province of the Austro-Hungarian Empire which became part of Romania after World War I. At that moment in history, Unitarianism referred to those who believed in the toleration of other faiths and the unity of God (as opposed to the dogma of the Trinity). Again, some meanings of the word go back to theological controversies in the church that were settled—more or less—by the decisions of the famous Council of Nicaea in 325.

Other chapters in this *Pocket Guide* deal with contemporary meanings of Unitarianism and Universalism. But we note that the meanings have never stood still for long. It has been central to our tradition to understand truth as an evolving, growing reality and to understand that no one person, church, science, or generation can grasp the whole of truth or define it once and for all.

Our churches have existed and our beliefs have been foreshadowed in different places and at different times. Michael Servetus was perhaps the earliest of the Reformation anti-Trinitarians. He bore the unique distinction of being burned in effigy by the Roman Catholics and in actuality by the Protestants. He was burned at the stake in Geneva in 1553 with his great theological opus, *The Restitution of Christianity*, tied to his thigh.

In his book *Hunted Heretic*, Roland Bainton writes that Servetus "brought together in a single person the Renaissance and the left wing of the Reformation. He was at once a disciple of the Neoplatonic Academy at Florence and of the Anabaptists. The scope of his interests and accomplishments exhibits . . . the 'universal man' of the Renaissance, for Servetus was proficient in medicine, geography, biblical scholarship, and theology. In him, the most diverse tendencies of the Renaissance and the Reformation were blended." Clearly, he was among those radical theologians who stressed the union of the human and divine.

Our connections with the Renaissance have been underscored also by the Unitarian Universalist historian Arnold Crompton, who, in an earlier edition of this *Pocket Guide*, wrote:

> Under the still powerful influence of the Renaissance, scholar preachers in the university towns of Florence, Bologna, and Padua practiced complete freedom of inquiry. They appealed to conscience and reason as

> they searched the Scriptures. Some of these scholar preachers, such as Bernadino Ochino [we might add Faustus Socinus, Camilio Renato, and Sebastian Castellio], reached a Unitarian Universalist position not unlike that of American Universalists George de Benneville and Hosea Ballou in the eighteenth and early nineteenth centuries.

In 1565 Giorgio Biandrata, a refugee from Italy, founded the first anti-Trinitarian church in Poland. Faustus Socinus, an Italian like Biandrata, became the leader of the Polish anti-Trinitarians who were then known as Socinians. Ferenz David (known in the West as Francis David), who moved from Catholicism through Lutheranism and Calvinism to Unitarianism, became the great leader of the Transylvanian Unitarians. He was martyred in 1579, but the Unitarian churches he founded have remained strong to this day.

Unitarianism and Universalism Come to America

In England, the beginnings of Unitarianism are associated with John Biddle, who was often persecuted and imprisoned for his Unitarian beliefs. He died in prison in 1662. Joseph Priestley, the discoverer of oxygen, was a major figure in eighteenth-century English Unitarianism. Both a Unitarian minister and a scientist, he voiced radical theological and political views and sympathized with the aims of the American and the French revolutions. In 1791, his meeting house and laboratory were destroyed by a mob outraged by his views. In 1794 Priestly immigrated to America and gave a series of lectures in the Universalist Church in Philadelphia when that city was still the capital of the United States. A number of leaders in the new nation attended these lectures, including Priestley's friend Thomas Jefferson. The lectures led to the founding of the First Unitarian Church of Philadelphia, the first permanently established church in the United States to take the Unitarian name.

Priestley had immigrated to Pennsylvania in 1794. Fifty-three years earlier, in 1741, George de Benneville, an important figure in early American Universalism, had come to the same state. De Benneville was a lay preacher and a physician. In his boyhood, he had become convinced of the truth of Universalism. As a result of this conviction, he was ostracized by the French Protestant Church in England when he was fourteen.

Prior to coming to America, de Benneville preached the doctrine of universal salvation in Germany, England, Holland, and France. He was imprisoned in France and was saved from the guillotine by the intervention of King Louis XV. When he came to America, he was warmly welcomed by Pennsylvania pietist groups such as the Dunkers, the Universal Baptists, and the Quakers.

In the opinion of the Unitarian Universalist minister and historian Clinton Lee Scott, George de Benneville is entitled to be called the founder of American Universalism. In *The Universalist Church of America: A Short History*, Scott reminds us,

> When Universalists today emphasize individual freedom of belief, the unrestricted use of reason, religion as a way of living, human beings and their welfare as central in organized life, truth as the only authority, the nurture of the inner spirit, and the Bible as one of the many forms of revelation, they are stressing principles which were central to the faith of the Spiritual Reformers. To leave this heritage out of consideration is to render difficult the understanding of the Universalism of the present day.

Of course these words apply to Unitarian Universalism as a whole. The past and the present have an organic, dynamic, living relationship to each other.

In 1759, *Union*, an important statement on Universalism by James Relly, was published in England. It became a target for ministers who were out looking for heretics. A young man named John Murray heard Methodist ministers attacking Relly and resolved to approach him in person and bring the light to this heretic. But when he got to Relly, the tables were turned. James Relly proved to be a man of good conscience and strong persuasive powers. He convinced Murray of the soundness of the Universalist position. Murray became a Universalist.

Time spent in debtors' prison and the death of his wife and baby motivated Murray to come to America. It was not his intention to preach Universalism in his new country, but circumstances, as well as the depth of his beliefs, decreed otherwise. In 1770, he landed at Good Luck Point on Barnegat Bay, NJ, and was offered hospitality by Thomas Potter, a Universalist. At Potter's urging, Murray began to preach again. In 1779 he organized one of the first Universalist churches in America at Gloucester, MA. There, a group led by the merchant Winthrop Sargent, father of Judith Sargent Murray, had been studying Relly's *Union*. They invited John Murray to be their minister. Together, in 1786, they won a key legal battle for religious freedom in Massachusetts—the right to support the church and minister of their own choosing rather than pay taxes to support the congregationalist churches of the Standing Order.

Universalism had been developing in America even before Murray's arrival. There were de Benneville's efforts in Pennsylvania, along with Pennsylvania's radical spiritualists. Also, in the hill country of western Massachusetts and southern New Hampshire and Vermont, several congregations had broken away from the Baptists over the issue of universal salvation. The earliest leaders were Isaac Davis, August Streeter, and Caleb Rich, the latter organizing the first society of Universalists in 1773 in Warwick, MA. With his limitless energy and his courage to spread the hopeful message of universal salvation in the face of the widely accepted, orthodox doctrine of eternal damnation for sinners, Murray emerged, however, as the main catalyst of a larger movement. He brought several of the first churches and leaders together in 1785 at Oxford, MA, including the Rev. Elhanan Winchester of Philadelphia. Their purpose was to organize this new denomination in order to bolster their legal struggle for religious freedom. They met yearly after that, and in 1790 leaders from several states gathered in Philadelphia to adopt a "Rule of Faith" and take a stand to "put an end to all wars" and slavery.

Although some of the oldest roots of our Unitarian and Universalist movements can be traced to Pennsylvania in the second half of the eighteenth century, major events leading to the organizing of American Unitarianism and Universalism took place in New England. Early in the eighteenth century, there were ministers in the Congregational churches who sowed the seeds of a more rational and liberal interpretation of the Christian faith. These men were characterized by great breadth of mind and spirit. Among them were Ebenezer Gay, who took a liberal stand on the doctrine of the Trinity as early as 1740, and Charles Chauncy and Jonathan Mayhew of Boston.

Chauncy, minister of the First Church in Boston, became a leader of the liberal Unitarians in the Congregationalist movement and wrote a book near the end of his life in 1787 defending universal salvation. Along with his younger colleague Jonathan Mayhew, minister of the West Church in Boston, Chauncy was an early supporter of liberty for the American colonies. Mayhew became the most eloquent early spokesperson and thinker for political and religious liberty in the colonies during the developing revolution. These men remained tied to the Congregationalists. But as the years wore on, the Congregationalists proved unwilling to tolerate the growing number of Unitarians, whose ministers were mostly graduates of the liberal Harvard College.

Organizing the Movements

William Ellery Channing, minister of the Federal Street Church in Boston and one of the greatest figures in American Unitarian history, emerged as the leader of the liberal Congregationalists. A sermon that he delivered in 1819 in Baltimore, MD, became the rallying point for a new liberal religious movement and led to the organization of the American Unitarian Association. The controversy affected many of the oldest churches in New England; out of the twenty-five oldest, twenty soon took the Unitarian position. In all, approximately 125 churches became Unitarian and either withdrew or were forced from the Congregational denomination. These churches were led by men and women very much at home in the scientific and literary currents of the day. Their ministers were for the most part Harvard-educated.

With the Universalists, it was not a question of large numbers of strong, established churches banding together to form a new denomination. Ministers like Caleb Rich, John Murray, Elhanan Winchester, and Hosea Ballou drew into new congregations men and women who, like the Unitarians within Congregationalism, sought a more liberal interpretation of Christianity. They came from different denominations. A very large number came from the Baptists and some from the Methodists. They were for the most part self-educated, less affluent and more representative of the people at large than the Unitarians of the period. In 1894, the Universalists made the Universalist General Convention their national governing body, and in 1942 they adopted the name The Universalist Church in America. The American Unitarian Association was organized in 1825.

While the Unitarians stressed free will and the potential goodness of persons, the Universalists put more emphasis on God as love. This led to the humorous but pertinent remark of the nineteenth-century figure Thomas Starr King, son of a Universalist minister, who, during his brief but brilliant ministry, had served both Universalist and Unitarian churches: "The one [Universalists] thinks God is too good to damn them forever, and the other [Unitarians] thinks they are too good to be damned forever."

It is important to remember that our movement was born during a revolutionary period, and that the humanistic values of the period saturated the lives of our late eighteenth- and early nineteenth-century forebears. The links we had with the American Revolution are many. Suffice it to say that most of the signers of the Declaration of Independence were what we would today call "religious liberals."

One of our most precious inheritances is our congregational polity which came to us from the Congregational churches and other churches of the free spirit. From the beginning it was accepted that ultimate decision-making power rests in the hands of the individual, autonomous churches. Local congregations select and ordain their ministers, determine their forms of worship or celebration, set their own requirements—or lack of requirements—for membership, and are responsible for all aspects of church government.

We have already seen that our beliefs change over the generations and that the beliefs of individuals differ within the same generation and the same congregation. One way to catch a glimpse of the ways in which our beliefs have changed and of the spirit and attitudes that unite us, is to go directly to the words of those who set us on our way. Fortunately, what might be called the founding declarations have been brought together in two highly readable, well-edited books. *Universalism in America: A Documentary History*, edited by Ernest Cassara, opens with a historical sketch and then presents selections from Universalist writings. Beginning with the writings of George de Benneville, it concludes with those of a contemporary Unitarian Universalist minister and poet, Kenneth L. Patton. A similar work, *The Epic of Unitarianism: Original Writings from the History of Liberal Religion*, edited by David B. Parke, begins with selections from the writings of Michael Servetus and concludes with selections from the contemporary Unitarian Universalist scholar, theologian, and social reformer, James Luther Adams.

Opening Up Our Faith

Olympia Brown, suffragist pioneer in municipal reform, was ordained by the Northern (New York) Universalist Association in 1863. She is thus often spoken of as the first denominationally ordained woman minister in the United States. In his bicentennial historical essay on American Universalism, George Hunston Williams, retired Professor of Ecclesiastical History at Harvard University, writes, "Perhaps the most conspicuous feature of the Centennial Convention (the Universalist Centennial Convention held in Gloucester, MA, in 1870) was the prominence of women in the Universalist cause." Most prominent was Judith Sargent Murray, an early American feminist writer. Of the Unitarians, Margaret Fuller, author of *Women in the Nineteenth Century,* is perhaps the best known. To be a member of this company is to know that Unitarian Universalism is always reaching out and striving for greater understanding and inclusiveness.

Unitarians in Canada, by Phillip Hewett, minister emeritus of the Unitarian Church of Vancouver, British Columbia, was published in 1978. With scholarship, wit, and insight, Hewett describes the role Unitarians have played in Canadian life for more than 150 years. He brings to life our recent as well as more distant history within and outside Canada. His is one of a number of books published in the last decade that remind us of the depth and strength of our roots. The Unitarian Church in Montreal (Church of the Messiah) was organized in 1842, but the presence of Unitarians in the city had been known to the public as early as 1821. The Universalist Unitarian Church of Halifax was organized as a Universalist Church in 1843. The 1827 census listed fifty-five Universalists living in Nova Scotia. The First Unitarian Congregation of Toronto was organized in 1845. The Canadian Unitarian Council—Counseil Unitaire Canadien—was organized in 1961.

The Nineteenth Century and Beyond

In the 1830s, Unitarianism gave birth to the American cultural and religious movement known as Transcendentalism. This "New England Renaissance" gave a great impetus to American arts and philosophy. It influenced such writers as Emerson, Thoreau, Fuller, Hawthorne, Melville, Dickinson, and Whitman, to name the best known. Emerson, who was a Unitarian minister before branching out in his writing and lecturing, was one of the prime movers. He referred to Transcendentalism as "Idealism." Today we look back upon it as the beginning of a naturalism that sees the religious as centered in the everyday experiences in the world.

Transcendentalists stressed the unity and miracle of daily life transcending the dualism of spirit and body, heaven and earth—as embodied in Whitman's poetry. This natural mysticism helped deepen the social activism at the center of our religious movement. In the years preceding the Civil War, much of the energy of Unitarians and Universalists in the

United States was taken up with large issues such as the abolition of slavery, the emancipation of women, and the preservation of the Union.

After the war, it gradually became clear to Unitarians and Universalists that their survival and vibrancy depended on their capacity to bring their members together and find a stronger, renewed sense of conviction within each church as a whole. Twelve thousand Universalists gathered in a General Convention in Gloucester, MA, in 1870 to celebrate the centennial of John Murray's arrival in America. In a fascinating bicentennial essay published by the Universalist Historical Society in 1971, George Hunston Williams observes that in that 1870 General Convention, "Universalism completed the overhaul of its ecclesiastical structure, as did many other denominations after the Civil War, adopting a comprehensive new constitution for a uniform organization of the Universalist Church."

It has been a chronic problem for both Unitarians and Universalists to reconcile their love of individual freedom and autonomy with the necessity of church structures. There has been a strong bias against any kind of organization (particularly *denominational*), structure, or consensus on belief. In 1884, at a meeting of the National Conference of Unitarians, an event of great importance took place. The Unitarians transformed the American Unitarian Association from an association of individuals who paid annual dues of one dollar for voting privileges into an association of autonomous churches. This was done through the leadership of Henry W. Bellows, minister of the First Unitarian Church of New York City (now All Souls). Bellows was an organizing genius. During the Civil War, he had organized the United States Sanitary Commission to serve the war-wounded. Thomas Starr King, a close friend of Bellows, raised large amounts of money from wealthy California for war relief and also helped begin a movement toward closer relations between the Unitarian and Universalists.

Our history teaches us that institutions, ideas, and beliefs are measured by the lives they help us lead. The Unitarians and Universalists have had an excellent record in applying religious principles to the welfare of the world. Some of our activists include Susan B. Anthony, pioneer in the struggle for women's rights and anti-slavery leader; Adin Ballou, radical pacifist, severe critic of the injustices of capitalism, founder of Hopedale; Clara Barton, organizer of the American Red Cross; Henry Bergh, one of the founders of the American Society for the Prevention of Cruelty to Children; Dorothea Dix, crusader for the reform of institutions for the mentally ill; Samuel Gridley Howe, pioneer in work with the blind; Horace Greeley, crusading newspaper editor, champion of labor unions and cooperatives; Thomas Starr King, minister of the First Unitarian Church of San Francisco, who helped save California for the Union through his powerful oratory and who, along with Father Junipero Serra, represents California in the Hall of Fame in Washington, DC; Abner Kneeland, advocate of land reform, public education, birth control, commune living; Judith Sargent Murray and Margaret Fuller, intellectuals, essayists, and early feminists; Theodore Parker, abolitionist; and Joseph Tuckerman, pioneer social worker.

There were probably no denominations in nineteenth-century America that had more of a humanitarian impact on society than the Unitarians and Universalists. This activism has continued into the twentieth century. John Haynes Holmes, minister of the Community Church of New York City, an outspoken pacificist during World War I, was a co-founder of both the American Civil Liberties Union and the National Association for the Advancement of Colored People. He and Clarence Skinner, Dean of our Universalist Theological School at Tufts University, helped start the so-called Community Church movement, which stresses social activism and ecumenicity. Jane Addams, celebrated social worker; John Dewey, signer of the Humanist Manifesto; Adlai Stevenson, politician; Whitney Young, Urban League leader; Sophia Lyon Fahs, pioneer in religious education; Stephen Fritchman, courageous minister of the First Unitarian Church of Los Angeles; and Dana Greeley, first president of the Unitarian Universalist Association and champion of civil rights number among our most renowned figures. This is not to say that this road has been easy, or that there has been unanimity (unanimity has never been our strong point). But these reformers have represented the cutting edge. They have demonstrated that our religion is a powerful motivating force for both personal growth and social change.

It has not been our custom to reflect often on our history. We tend to be in a hurry to get things done and look forward rather than backward. But stopping to look at our past is reassuring, renewing, and energizing. It can also give us a sense of who we are, open up our minds to new ideas, and encourage us to deepen our religious life. Our story is adventurous and full of hope. Since Unitarian Universalists have attempted to keep alive the core teachings and beliefs of what has been called "the perennial religion," our leaders have often been faced with persecution and charges of heresy, in the tradition of the prophets and seers of all ages. Discovering the depth and strength of these roots of ours is a nourishing experience that gives us the inspiration and stamina we need to meet today's great challenges.

Harry Scholefield and Paul Sawyer

Our Ministry

Defining the ministry is not as easy for Unitarian Universalists as it is for the young woman in Gail Godwin's story *Father Melancholy's Daughter*. In that novel, the child of a clergyperson speaks of ministry in very concrete terms:

> It was curious, this business of being [a minister]. You were the star; nobody but you could wear the gorgeous vestments . . . or preach the sermon but at the same time you were always having to ask permission and plead for your spending money . . . and worry about causing gossip or offending people.

The first definition of "ministry" in the dictionary refers not to a calling but to an attitude. It is, according to *Webster's*, "the *act* of ministering or serving." When Unitarian Universalists speak of ministry, we are describing what we all do together as members of our faith communities. We have ordained ministers in our tradition, of course, but those who serve their world in the name of the church extend far beyond the clergy. As people who have chosen to join in a shared religious venture, all Unitarian Universalists contribute to the efforts we call ministry.

Our Faith Communities

With more than one thousand to their number, Unitarian Universalist congregations cannot be typecast. We have some congregations that consist of a handful of people, some whose membership hovers around one hundred, and some whose congregants total ten times that number. We have some groups that call themselves "churches," and some have named themselves "fellowships." We have congregations *with* ministers and some *without*. Our faith communities have the authority to select clergy for ourselves but some choose to have no ordained leaders, preferring to remain lay-led. Though we are a diverse population, a common truth for Unitarian Universalist communities remains: regardless of the size or constellation of the congregation, the ministry in our faith communities is mutual.

The Sufi sect, an ancient Islamic group of mystics, have long recognized this type of ministry. They honored the human need for mutual caretaking of one another when they first began singing these words, a chant that has endured through the generations: "From you I receive, to you I give, together we share, from this we live." Other religions have also spoken of the need to minister to one another. Perhaps no other story depicts so vividly our longing for friends to stick by us in times of despair than the ancient story of Job, found in Hebrew Scripture.

When God's good and faithful servant survives catastrophe after catastrophe, when he meets one crisis after another with no reprieve whatsoever, some friends come to visit him. They offer unsolicited advice and pose unsolicited theories as to why Job is experiencing such bad luck. Finding their words unhelpful, Job finally tells his friends what he needs of them:

> Listen to me, do but listen,
> and let that be the comfort you offer me.
> Bear with me while I have my say;
> When I have finished, you may mock.
> May not I too voice my thoughts?
> Have I not as good cause to be impatient?
> Look at my plight, and be aghast;
> clap your hand to your mouth.
>
> —Job 21:1-5
> New English Bible

The need for giving and receiving help is recognized in many religious traditions. It is what we do in our faith communities.

We give and receive assistance when we gather in adult education classes and listen to one another's religious questions and share our own stories of success or struggle. We engage in mutual ministry when we offer ourselves as mentors to our youth and speak to our children about our deepest values. We model community caring when we help one another during times of crisis by baking a casserole or offering a ride, by holding a hand or giving a hug.

As people of faith, our ministry involves taking care of one another, maintaining an emotional and spiritual connection throughout life's changes. As we engage in mutual ministry, we feed one another. And in so doing, we are able in turn to lend our succor to the world. Our pastoral presence, our religious education, and our social action are all grounded in the ministry we give to and receive from one another.

When Unitarian Universalists are talking about ministry, we are talking about our faith communities.

Our Lay Leadership

Unitarian Universalists believe in the power of partnership between layperson and professional minister because we believe that each of us has something to offer to this world. We see the job of the ordained clergy as defining only one part of our ministry. "Do not think that saintliness comes from occupation," said Meister Eckert more than 600 years ago.

Though ministers are rarely confused with saints, they are, in some traditions, regarded as the specially sanctified. Eckert reminds us that the work which we each do can be viewed as venerable. Religious work depends less on job title than on effort and intent. He writes:

> The kind of work we do does not make us holy but we may make it holy. However "sacred" a calling may be, as it is a calling, it has no power to sanctify; but rather we are and have the divine being within; we bless each task we do.

The leaders in our congregations are both lay and ordained. Respect for the contributions and authority of the laity is genuine. Our history is replete with people who have inspired those who surround them. There are those who are famous, whose names are well-known to the world, and there are those whose impact is subtler.

Our Association has long been nurturing of its lay leadership. We have committed resources to the support and training of lay leaders on regional and continental levels. Workshops about every aspect of church life abound at our annual Association gathering, the General Assembly. Over the years, leadership schools designed to develop the skills and talents of the laity have been offered throughout the continent. Many congregations have programs in place that offer guidance and support to their own leaders.

Our lay leaders are Board chairpersons as well as committee workers. They are Directors of Religious Education and choir members. They are our treasurers and ushers. They arrange our coffee hours and organize our bazaars. The opportunities to be a leader in our congregations are limitless.

Who each of us is in this world is the gift we bring to our mutual ministry. Our strengths and successes, our fears and vulnerabilities are what we have to offer. For decades Catholic theologian Henri Nouwen has provided people with potent images of what true ministry is. He has said that all of us can and do serve and nurture others by being authentic about and true to our life experiences. We are all, in his words, "wounded healers." "The great mystery of ministry," he says, "is that while we ourselves are overwhelmed by our own weaknesses and limitations, we can still be so transparent that the Spirit of God, the divine counselor, can shine through us and bring light to others."

There could be no ministry without the commitment and involvement of the laity. When Unitarian Universalists are talking about ministry, we are speaking about our lay leaders.

Our Religious Professionals

A classicist might view the role of the clergy as pastor, prophet, rabbi, or preacher. Familiar as these concepts are to Unitarian Universalist ministers, more modern metaphors could also be woven into our understandings of the ordained. Clergy are also storytellers, midwives, and jugglers.

As storytellers, we relate the tales of the past, present, and future to the people around us. Our task is to describe as clearly as we can the ways of the world and its people. The pastoral stories are related when we are counseling people in our offices or on the telephone. Prophetic tales are told when we speak out against the wrongs we see in the world and offer a vision of what could be. We are being priestly when we honor the stories of important religious rituals, such as marriage or child dedication. Ministers are rabbis when we share the traditions of our religious heritage. We are preachers when we speak stories from our own lives.

As midwives, we help give birth to the life abiding within the congregation. It is not our place to take credit for what is created. It is not we who breathe life into what emerges; we merely assist in the delivery. This occurs in Sunday worship—as well as in small group sharings, staff meetings, in congregational meetings, and in our work with both adults and children. Our job is to know when to step aside and let nature take its course and when to intervene with special care.

As jugglers, we try to make order out of chaos. We keep an eye on all the activities around us, on all the participants before us, and on all the moods within us. In private moments with parishioners and in public forums with the congregation, we are asked to hold in tension a multitude of truths. With hands and heart, we try to bring balance to the sometimes conflicting needs in our faith communities.

The Unitarian Universalist Association speaks of three distinct types of ordained ministry: parish ministers, ministers of religious education, and community ministers. Each of these professionals is called to be pastor, prophet, priest, rabbi, preacher, storyteller, midwife, and juggler.

The parish minister attends to the myriad needs of a gathered congregation. As men and women, we are professionals who covenant with our communities to join together in the religious journey and to be attentive to all that occurs along the way. This job entails being both a leader and a participant in the life of the church. There are countless ways to characterize parish ministry, but perhaps the most accurate description is one offered by the Rev. Gary Smith. The task of the parish minister, he says, is in part "to articulate, on behalf of all of us, the substance of faith that can both comfort and confront, both nurture and inspire."

The minister of religious education focuses on the educational growth of Unitarian Universalists. These ministers pay particular attention to the programs that enhance self-knowledge and personal understanding of the religious in life. These professionals are committed to the religious development of both children and adults. One minister of religious education says, "We are concerned with ministering to people where they are." The Rev. Margaret Corletti adds, "We need to think in the context of ministering to every age in a way that is enlightening and nurturing and supportive, regardless of where you are in your spiritual journey."

Some of our larger churches are served by both a parish minister and a minister of religious education.

The community minister is concerned with serving the needs of our larger society. Though many Unitarian Universalist clergy have devoted their careers to just such service, the formal recognition of this particular ministry is relatively new. Some community ministers serve inner city neighborhoods. Others serve particular populations that have long been abandoned and marginalized—such as rape victims, the homeless, and the imprisoned. All have answered a deep call to be responsive to the plights of our world.

The Rev. Donald E. Robinson, one of the first Unitarian Universalists to be fellowshipped for community ministry, speaks with passion about his calling: "You have to bring the program to the people. You can't do it alone. You have to build a network." Don speaks of the responsibility established congregations have to help make community ministry work. He sees crucial connections between parish work and community work. "Community ministry helps to express in actions the values church members profess to believe," Don says. "It helps each person develop a religion for living."

The academic training for each type of ministry is the same. All our ministers must have earned a Master of Divinity degree or its equivalent from an accredited theological school. There are three that are affiliated with our Association: Meadville/Lombard Theological School in Chicago, IL; Starr King School for the Ministry in Berkeley, CA; and Harvard Divinity School in Cambridge, MA. Over half of our ordained ministers are trained at one of these schools; the rest attend various Protestant seminaries. Some of our ministers of religious education earn their academic credentials through Meadville/Lombard's Independent Study Program.

The professional credentialing arm of our Association is known as the Ministerial Fellowship Committee. This group consists of ordained ministers and laypersons; they review, evaluate, and certify all our professional ministers. The final authority for investing our leaders as ministers, however, rests with our faith communities. It is the congregation which ordains the minister.

Unitarian Universalist clergy come in both sexes, represent a variety of ages, and offer an array of life experiences. Though our ministers can't be drawn in one brush stroke, described with one gesture, or contained in one image, one truth can be spoken of us all. We are here to be in the world and with the world through all of its rhythms. We share with others in times of celebration, times of despair, and in all times that lie between.

Our ordained ministers—parish ministers, ministers of religious education, and community ministers—stand with the priest in Henry Wadsworth Longfellow's poem *Evangeline*. At the story's end, the people are being deported from their homeland to various and unknown countries. The action, cruel and politically motivated, shows no regard for family ties or legacies. Children are separated from their parents, lovers and spouses are pulled apart from one another. Through this wretched turmoil, the parish priest tries his best to help his beloved people. In the end, all he can offer is his hand and his heart, his tears and his love.

> Onward from fire to fire as from hearth to hearth in his parish,
> Wandered the faithful priest, consoling and blessing and cheering . . .
> Thus he approached the place where Evangeline sat with her father,
> And in the flickering light beheld the face of the old man,
> Haggard and hollow and wan, and without either thought or emotion
> E'en as the face of a clock from which the hands have been taken . . .
> 'Benedicte!' murmured the priest, in tones of compassion.
> More he fain would have said, but his heart was full, and his accents
> Faltered and paused on his lips, as the feet of a child on a threshold,
> Hushed by the scene he beholds, and the awful presence of sorrow.
> Silently, therefore, he laid his hand on the head of the maiden,
> Raising his eyes, full of tears, to the silent stars that above them
> Moved on their way, unperturbed by the wrongs and sorrows of mortals.
> Then sat he down at her side, and they wept together in silence.

It is all of us—members of faith communities, lay leaders, and religious professionals—who join in the spirit of the old Sufi song: "From you I receive, to you I give, together we share, from this we live."

Beth Graham

Our Worship

"O thou beautiful . . . radiance. There is no day nor night, nor form nor color, and never, never a word."

This luminous line from *Gitanjali* was written by Rabindranath Tagore, winner of the 1913 Nobel Prize in literature. Tagore wrote his evocative poems in Bengali and often translated them into English himself. I'd like to think that Tagore's religious community, the Brahmo Somaj, which was influenced by nineteenth-century Unitarianism, nourished the spiritual depth of his poetry. The Nobel committee was so taken with the poetry's depth that one of them urged his fellows to learn Bengali to better appreciate the original. I find Tagore's poetry, especially his *Gitanjali*, to be quite compelling expressions of the awe I see at the center of the concept of worship.

Awe? The sense of awe that hums in a mother holding her firstborn for the first time. The sense of awe that shivers in a young man whose glimpse of the night sky suggests both his significance and his insignificance. The sense of awe echoing in an older woman who suddenly grasps the meaning of her own mortality. The sense of awe that affects true friends in the heat of an honest conversation. The sense of awe that kindles the heart of a man when he watches the morning sun strike his bedroom wall and realizes how glad he is to be alive in that moment, free of past or future.

In short "awe" is the word I use to describe what seizes me when I realize that I live at all, that everything *is*, that hope is possible, that limits are to be expected, that tragedy is real, that control is largely an illusion—but that love is nonetheless desirable. The ancient and very rich word "worship" well describes my response to that awe: a sense of amazement, a sense of profound gratitude or acceptance, even a bodily trembling. Most often this kind of worship is both solitary and involuntary. I'd guess it is the most common sort of worship in the world, no matter the faith or doubt of the worshipper. Some folks may come to conclusions about God, I suppose, but for the most part, those who know this kind of worship say, with Tagore, "never, never a word."

Worship in Community

Worship has another, more limited meaning, however, which concerns us here. Worship may also describe non-solitary and quite voluntary experiences of artful celebration designed for congregations of *any* Western religious tradition. The Holy Communion at St. John's Lutheran Church, Friday evening Shabbat service over at Temple Beth Shalom, Christmas midnight Mass down at All Saints, and Morning Celebration at Starr King Unitarian Universalist Church are several of the names our spiritual traditions give this other kind of worship. Unitarian Universalists call this time the "service," "Morning Worship," the "Sunday Program," or just plain "worship." Though the content, style, or touchstones of Unitarian Universalist worship will differ from worship in a Friends' Meetinghouse, Greek Orthodox Church, Reconstructionist Synagogue, or American Buddhist Church, all denominations share the idea of special times, particular ways to structure those times, and the central value of the gathered community. As with every other spiritual group, Unitarian Universalists range in our worship from plain to fancy, from "low church" to "high church," from singular to eclectic. There is no uniform style of worship, no agreed upon pattern of artful celebration among us.

The same is true of setting. Unitarian Universalists gather on Sunday in large rented homes, in striking modern buildings, in whitewashed New England meetinghouses, and in Gothic chapels splashed with the turquoise of stained glass. I know of one congregation that meets in a sort of outdoor amphitheater by the sea and another that meets in a converted barn. In these varied settings, you may find 600 parishioners gathered before a high pulpit or fifteen people sitting on simple wooden chairs in a neon-lit room.

In most of these settings the worship celebration usually lasts for about an hour. On rare evening occasions, such as the ordination of a new minister, the service may take longer. A midweek chapel, on the other hand, might last only thirty minutes. At a celebration like an ordination, you might see robes of rich color and elaborate rituals, such as the laying on of hands. At a regular Sunday celebration, you may see no gowns at all. Very often you will find that leaders of worship wear their finest daily clothes, and you will find the ritual to be relatively spare.

The Order of Worship

In most of our congregations there will be an *Order of Service*, a printed brochure that outlines the structure of celebration as practiced by that particular set of people. Musical preludes or chimes of some sort often begin our services of worship, calling us to attention and initial reflection. Opening words or invocations spoken by a minister or lay leader help us to remember how common worship is connected to our experiences of private awe. Sometimes a choir or the congregation will sing a verse of praise, often called a doxology. Longer hymns or songs of praise to the morning—or to Spirit, to Life, or to Love—are often sung close to the beginning of a service. Also at this point, a fire is often kindled in a wide-brimmed chalice. This ancient symbol of our living tradition reminds us that we are neither the first nor the last persons who so gather. Other congregations light candles "of memory and of hope."

Our children very often help to begin our worship celebrations. A story, a skit, a brief homily "to the child in all of us" will sometimes set the tone for the whole rest of the hour. Sometimes the whole morning is intergenerational.

In the middle of our worship celebrations fall a variety of devotional and community-building activities. Longer silences are sometimes introduced by a bell sound; prayers or meditations from the pulpit (or from the order of service) are sometimes read alone or with the group; image-rich guided meditations are sometimes included in the service. These devotions offer us room to mesh our common, structured experience of worship with the memory of our unstructured, personal experience of awe. In them, we are often invited to remember the whole of our lives, our losses as well as our joys, our desire to grow deeper as well as our desire to be affirmed just as we are. In them, many discern Spirit, named or unnamed.

Recently, some of our congregations have developed rituals around the passages in ordinary human life: the birth of a grandchild, the passing of an exam, the loss of an uncle, the visit of good friends, a divorce or an engagement. Sometimes involving the lighting of candles and telling of personal stories, sometimes involving the naming of loved ones in the middle of a silent meditation, such rituals of "joys and concerns" may serve to deepen real bonds of community. Some congregations set aside a Sunday each month to memorialize with candles those who have died, a kind of Unitarian Universalist version of the Jewish *Kaddish*. This openness to grief as well as joy surprises some visitors to our congregations. But though many Unitarian Universalists use Von Ogen Vogt's useful phrase "Celebration of Life" as a compact definition of worship, no one would understand the word "celebration" as lifting up only the happier moments of life. Without a genuine depth and an honest wholeness, group worship can flatten out like foil—shiny, but without weight.

Music as Celebration

After the devotional period, choirs may then sing an anthem. From a North American folk tune such as *What Wondrous Love* accompanied on an autoharp to a portion of Leonard Bernstein's exhilarating *Chichester Psalms*, the choral anthem is often a brilliant portion of the service. Moreover, the swell of a great pipe organ resonating a Bach fugue during morning service might well offer the whole meaning of worship to some hearts. String quartets may delight us with Ives, soloists with the jazz style perfected by Odetta. Some of our congregations are developing dance choirs to reinforce the truth that worship is as much an action of the body as a direction of the mind. Several of our smaller congregations get the whole congregation circle-dancing on special Sundays. There is a growing organization, the Unitarian Universalist Musicians' Network, which meets every summer to hone professional skills, exchange ideas, and encourage its members in the musical arts of worship. More and more, music in all of its forms reveals itself as a touchstone of Unitarian Universalist worship.

It is rare indeed to experience any worship among us without singing from the congregation. Whether the sound is thin and tentative or echoing off the rafters in four-part harmony, singing remains an essential element in Unitarian Universalist worship. For more than a hundred years, Universalists and Unitarians have enriched not just their own celebrations but the celebrations of other Western religious traditions as well. The hymnbooks *Hymns of the Spirit* (1937) and *Hymns for the Celebration of Life* (1964) collect congregational songs from many cultures and introduce stunning new texts. Both of these books had wide influence among other religious traditions. The most recent hymnbook of the Unitarian Universalists is called *Singing the Living Tradition* (1993). Spirituals, chants from South Africa, Jewish melodies, Chinese pentatonic tunes, six-part rounds, jazz pieces, and contemporary commissions from Alan Hovhaness and Dede Duson usher us into the wider world which we claim as our common home.

The words sung to these tunes are also revelatory. Originally, Unitarians and Universalists used hymns of the Christian tradition but with references to the Trinity and to hellfire removed or recast. But for the last hundred years, writers have been experimenting with fresher language in order to move closer to the center of our historic tradition. For example, Unitarian Universalists refer to the Divine in ways often more poetic than doctrinal. "Spirit of Life," "Life of Ages," "Life of Life"—phrases such as these evoke a lively view of the Holy and help us to keep idolatry at bay.

The Power of the Words

The Universalist insistence that salvation is for everyone, not just "the elect," now takes its practical form in the power of language to signify inclusion. "In the beginning was the Word" —so begins the hymn taken from the Gospel of John. This

"Word," according to early liberal theologians in Alexandria, was "the reason" on which all the goodness of Creation was modeled. Similarly, modern students of language recognize the Word's creative power to shape the world. Thus, exclusively masculine language tends to create a world where only men's beliefs, ways, and stories are valued . . . and fifty percent of the human race becomes invisible. So, to safeguard "universal salvation," Unitarians and Universalists have been making the shared language of hymns and songs broader, more reflective of the actual realities of a dual-gender world. Thus, our hymns ought not be seen as artistic additions to the service but as true expressions of our religious sensibility. They do two amazing things. They express the reality that the earth is indeed inhabited by people of two genders, and they demand greater justice from all who sing of that reality.

There are other concerns, too. We live in a world where beige and brown people are rhetorically called "black" and "white," and where those called "white" claim a centrality denied to those called "black." Hymns which speak of every sin, every diabolical situation as "black" or "dark," and every grace or joy as "white" or "fair" or "of the light" seem to reflect the harmful rhetoric of a divided world. Unitarian Universalists who sing of the beauty of all colors not only receive traditions but also help to remold those traditions to help begin healing the world. It doesn't work like magic, but over time—and with humility of heart—it does work.

The Sermon

A Unitarian Universalist I know once asked me, "Who's doing so-and-so's ordination?" Somehow I knew he wasn't asking about who was leading the laying on of hands but about the preacher. It's not surprising. Sermons feature so prominently in our worship that sometimes people talk (albeit inaccurately) as if sermons and worship were synonymous.

Good preaching can sometimes threaten to eclipse other parts of a celebration. I've more often wept during sermons than during prayers or rituals. The sermon is often the only time I laugh during an entire service. These are compelling associations. I've also been bored or impatient during sermons. Sermons can be overdone. There have been times after I've preached when I've known at once that the silent meditation was far more meaningful than my confused words.

But a good sermon can provoke a decision that moves a person in a whole new direction. It can lift up a portion of our lives, holding it in just such a light as to reveal facets we couldn't easily see before. A good sermon (and there are many of them) can tug us further down the path toward a difficult forgiveness or remind us of our inestimable value as persons in a world that values little. Sermons can remind us of basic things we've forgotten, help us to learn and unlearn, show us how to reframe the seemingly impossible ideals so that we do not lose hope. I've heard sermons that have helped me question an easy faith, even wrestle with God.

Confessional preaching may invite us to be less tentative about our own truths. Prophetic preaching may rekindle a passion for justice on earth. Good preaching can bring us to the brink of awe no less than the evening star. A sermon may be read from a carefully crafted text or improvised after long mental preparation. It may be memorized or developed from notes. It may be long or short, prosaic or poetic. A sermon can be a dialogue between two people or a story acted out with dramatic props. In any case, the central part of most Unitarian Universalist worship is the sermon, the message, the homily, the talk. A bad sermon may not destroy a worship celebration, but a good sermon certainly enhances one.

Readings are often shared before a sermon, but sometimes they are incorporated into the text of the sermon. These readings may be from just about anywhere. Spiritual readings, both from ancient scripture and more modern sources, are certainly commonplace. But the morning newspaper may feature just as frequently. I also use poems from various cultures and selections from novels or plays. But whether a story from the Gospel of Mark or a poem by Marge Piercy, readings help to root us. They remind us that we neither invented religious liberalism nor do we complete it.

The Variety of Ritual

On certain Sundays you might experience rituals out of our taproot traditions, sacramental or symbolic events of soulful beauty. There may be a "breaking of bread," the ancient ritual of communion inclusively and freshly interpreted. A litany of *Kol Nidrei* may be sung during the Jewish High Holidays. Some of our congregations celebrate the Passover Seder in one form or another, Tenebrae on Good Friday, or the Eucharist on Maundy Thursday. The Flower Communion Festival, a moving ceremony involving cut flowers, is a common Unitarian Universalist practice held on Easter Sunday or in June. These tangible symbols often prove more significant than either the sermon or the devotions, perhaps because they more effectively address us as whole persons, as bodies and not as mere minds.

Although sermons and rituals often come toward the end of a service, the actual closing of a service usually features a hymn and a blessing or a set of closing words. Often a powerful musical postlude will conclude the celebration.

Some of our congregations do not take up an offering, but the greater number do. The offering, whatever else it may symbolize, is certainly a summons to support the institution that nurtures and encourages liberal thought in religion.

In a Unitarian Universalist congregation, anyone can write

a meditation, preach a sermon, or lead a worship celebration. Ordained ministers most often lead worship in our congregations, but lay members have also developed artful skills of celebration. A different quartet of lay members plans worship each week in at least one of our congregations. Most of our congregations seem to have at least one lay-led Sunday per month, when an individual or group plans worship.

Recently, some ministers have started working with a lay associate every Sunday. Guests may be invited; a Congresswoman may speak on how her Unitarian Universalist principles guide her decisions, or an astronomer may offer observations on the stars that help elucidate the connection between science and religion. Lest it appear that ordained ministers stick to "spiritual" topics while lay members explore the more secular ideas, I should point out that Thomas Starr King, one of our great nineteenth-century ministers, used to preach brilliant sermons based on such natural phenomena as comets. He even managed to find lessons in the science of metallurgy!

Rites of Passage

Unitarian Universalists join other religious folk in marking the great transitions in a human life—birth, coming-of-age, marriage or union, joining a church, covenanting with a new minister (ordination and installation), death and grieving—each may be celebrated with beauty, poignancy, and depth. It would be helpful to take a closer look at a few of these types of worship.

Marriages for men and women and rites of union for same-sex couples most often occur on weekends at times other than Sunday morning. These are rarely more than a half-hour long and may take a variety of forms, but some public exchange of the couple's consent is usually part of the ceremony.

A memorial or funeral service may involve many people speaking brief remembrances, as well as familiar poems and psalms and direct words about death and grief. These celebrations of peoples' lives vary in length and tone, but I have never left one unmoved.

Unlike weddings or memorial services, the Sunday morning worship most often proves the best setting for the naming of a baby. "Dedication," "naming," or "christening" are the most frequently used terms for such a rite. Godparents may or may not be involved. One common form of such a service involves a rosebud and clear water touched to the child's forehead. Others use water alone, but there is no thought here of a child being born in sin and needing to be washed. "With water, which is as clear as your spirit, my child, . . ." the minister intones. Some ministers use the four elements—earth, air, fire, and water—as blessings on the child's body, intellect, passions, and spirit. The forms are varied, but the joy in such a ceremony is always of a piece.

In *Gitanjali*, Rabindranath Tagore wrote, "The same stream of life that runs through my veins night and day runs through the world and dances in rhythmic measures." Tagore also saw the waves of the sea and every flowering branch or blade of grass as part of that living "stream of life." The stately dance of the seasons, the lifeblood of the body, the breaking forth of the spirit—all of these tributaries flow into a mighty river that summarizes in its perpetual movement the power of worship in the living tradition. Tagore asked, "Is it beyond you to be glad with the gladness of this rhythm?" This question is nothing less than an invitation to leave the superficial behind and to embrace the life of the Spirit.

Mark Belletini

Our Religious Education

The greatest gifts we can give our children, it is said, are "roots and wings." Unitarian Universalist religious education seeks to give us all, no matter what our ages, roots of connection and wings of possibility and hope. Our religious education is lifespan in scope, progressive in theory, experiential in method, and liberal in its theological and ethical perspectives.

The role of liberal religious education in this last decade of the twentieth century is to help individuals of all ages experience connections, compassion, and creativity. We need to understand our connection with our liberal religious heritage: the Jewish and Christian roots from which we spring; the Eastern religious traditions which have nurtured us; the insights of philosophy and science which have expanded our knowledge; and our mystical sense of union with one another, our planet, and the universe. We need to feel compassion and act upon it; to empathize with the struggles and joys which are a part of every life journey; to transform oppression into justice; to persevere on behalf of what is right. And finally, we need to encourage and unlock the creativity in each of us in order to utilize fully our individual gifts and, in so doing, to find new solutions to complex problems.

From the Reformation to the Twentieth Century

The roots of liberal religious education go back (as do the roots of liberal religion itself) to the Reformation. Martin Luther, writing in the sixteenth century, expressed his belief that children are more educable than older people. He showed a basic understanding of the development of the child's cognitive and emotional capacities, and he even suggested the use of games as teaching and learning aids.

In the seventeenth century, John Locke also planted seeds of liberal thinking about religious education. In *Some Thoughts Concerning Education*, published in 1693, Locke critiqued the form of religious education which had developed in the first century following the Reformation. He argued against using the Bible as a primary text for young children who could have no clear understanding of what it was about.

In the United States, the eighteenth century witnessed a division of thought as to the nature of the child and the type of education needed. The conservative Jonathan Edwards insisted that a child was by nature a hater of God and Goodness and could only become religious by an act of "divine violence" through which the human will was suddenly and miraculously recreated. Charles Chauncy, a liberal, believed that one came to a gradual understanding of religious truths. He did not agree that religious conversion was the only route to individual salvation and offered instead the possibility of growth through religious education.

Although such seeds of liberal religious education were present from the time of the Protestant Reformation, they did not take root for several centuries. The catechism was the educational method of choice for most Catholic and Protestant congregations. With this tool, religious doctrine was put in the form of questions and answers to be memorized by the students. There was no opportunity for the learner to question or explore alternative religious understandings.

The Sunday school movement began in England and the United States in the late eighteenth and early nineteenth centuries as an attempt to offer secular schooling to children who worked in factories the other six days of the week. Congregational churches in New England formed such schools and soon added the teaching of morals and religion to the curriculum. Some of these congregations became officially Unitarian in the early part of the nineteenth century. Universalist Sunday schools had their beginnings in Philadelphia in 1790, when Dr. Benjamin Rush helped found the "First Day" or "Sunday School Society."

In 1833, Henry Ware, Jr., made the first attempt to produce a curriculum for the Unitarian Sunday schools in the form of a series of books about the life and times of Jesus and the history of Christianity. In 1837, ten years after the formation of the Boston Sunday School Society (later to become the Unitarian Sunday School Society), the Rev. William Ellery Channing was asked to give the main address at the annual meeting. In his travels to England, Channing had become aware of more liberal approaches to education, and in his address he offered his co-religionists in Boston some truly revolutionary ideas. He declared that the Sunday school movement should be responsive to the needs and capacities of children. His eloquent words are still quoted today in many Unitarian Universalist religious education materials:

> The great end in religious instruction . . . is not to stamp our minds irresistibly on the young but to stir up their own; not to make them see with our eyes but to look inquiringly and steadily with their own; not to

> give them a definite amount of knowledge but to inspire a fervent love of truth; not to form an outward regularity but to touch inward springs. . . .

Unfortunately, Channing's vision was not put into actual practice for almost seventy-five years, until the "New Beacon Course in Religious Education" was created by the American Unitarian Association shortly after the turn of the twentieth century.

Process and Method

Liberal religious education in this century has focused as much on process and method as it has on content. Perhaps the two most prominent pioneers in this effort were Sophia Lyon Fahs, a Unitarian religious educator, and Angus MacLean, a Universalist minister and professor at St. Lawrence Theological School in Canton, NY.

Fahs came to Unitarianism from a Presbyterian family background. While working for a Master of Arts degree at the Teachers College of Columbia University in New York, she became involved in the experimental Sunday school at the College, which was based on progressive principles of education, particularly the work of John Dewey. It was here that she began to develop and articulate her vision for religious education.

Fahs believed in a naturalistic theism which utilized scientific knowledge and empirical process to understand and appreciate the mysteries of life. Her goal was to change "the conception of the educational process from one of indoctrination and acceptance of authority to one of creative discovery, intelligent examination, and free decision."

In 1931, she was asked to join a committee which was studying the curricula of the American Unitarian Association

(AUA). As a result of that experience, she was offered a position at the AUA as curriculum editor working with Ernest Kuebler, the new Secretary of the Department of Religious Education. Kuebler and Fahs instituted a new era not only in Unitarian religious education but in liberal religious education in general. The New Beacon Series they produced is still regarded as a milestone in the field. This curriculum was based on the principle that religious educators could facilitate a person's spiritual growth through interaction with carefully chosen materials and with the environment. It was not a "course of study" but more a guide to assist teachers and learners to grow together into an awareness of the spiritual meaning of living. Self-esteem, appreciation of others' values and experiences, shaping the person into a psychologically well-adjusted, emotionally healthy, socially conscious person were some of its progressive aims.

A very important Universalist who influenced liberal religious education during this time was Angus MacLean. MacLean was a professor of religious education at the Theological School of St. Lawrence University. He contributed to the atmosphere out of which the New Beacon Series arose.

For MacLean, "a religion that seeks to serve the living generation is the only one that can fully embrace all time." Past experience has value only in terms of present purpose. Education for MacLean was the process of continuous and creative sharing in the life of humankind. He believed that church school teachers needed to bring "more of the child's normal life into the school, more of [his or her] natural concerns and interests and more of the things to which the child's purpose and interest most easily attach themselves."

The process and methods used today continue to focus on materials appropriate to the developmental stage of the learner. There are stories and resources from a variety of religious and secular traditions. There are activities to help make the learnings come alive—from arts and crafts to music, drama, and dance. Learners are encouraged to question, to pull and tug at difficult problems and dilemmas. Different backgrounds, beliefs, and viewpoints are celebrated. There is also an invitation to share the vision and values articulated in our Unitarian Universalist Principles and Purposes. There is an attempt made to acknowledge and utilize a variety of learning styles in order that students feel affirmed, not inadequate. Teachers are encouraged to model a continuing search for greater understanding. There is awareness of the reality that religious education is truly a lifelong process. What then does this process and method offer to those who have chosen Unitarian Universalism as their religious path?

Connections

One of the most important things Unitarian Universalist religious education tries to offer its students of all ages is a sense of connection. This connection begins in infancy as the newborn child feels its bond to parents and family. The congregation's welcoming of the infant into a warm and inviting nursery atmosphere and its affirmation of the worth of each child in the Child Welcoming, or Dedication, Ceremony are ways of enlarging this bond from family to religious community. Programs for young children focus on strengthening feelings of self-worth and self-esteem as these youngsters start making friends outside the home. Introductions to our Unitarian Universalist congregations are done with care and creative techniques. Intergenerational events where people of all ages play and learn together are especially important and create a sense of connection with the entire religious community.

As the young child enters elementary school and progresses through the years of schooling toward high school, connections to other faiths are made—connections to our Jewish and Christian roots as well as to other world religions. How Unitarian Universalists utilize philosophy, the scientific method, and other intellectual traditions is also an important "religious" connection made in our curricula.

Our youth organization, Young Religious Unitarian Universalists (YRUU), serves youth from ages twelve to twenty. YRUU utilizes both curriculum materials as well as the interests of the teens themselves to determine the agenda for youth group meetings. In conjunction with their adult advisors, youth groups plan a variety of programs. These programs take the form of sessions on spirituality and religion to hands-on experiences with social justice projects to parties for fun and fellowship. Regional, district, and continental youth conferences offer our teenagers yet another way to connect with one another and with our larger movement.

The role of parents in religious education is critical.The hour of church school once a week is only a small window of opportunity in which to encourage religious growth. The real religious education takes place in the home, as children and youth observe how their elders live out their values and beliefs.

Adult education materials help adults—who may be new to the denomination or longtime Unitarian Universalists—grapple with defining their own beliefs. This is an integral part of the liberal religious enterprise. Many of our congregations are developing exciting local adult programming, which includes courses on world religions, liberal theology, Unitarian Universalist history, and topics of current ethical concern.

In our approach to religious education, we utilize the best understandings of human development—cognitive, emotional, and religious. We explore how new findings about the human brain can help break down old blocks of prejudice. We reach for new techniques in learning theory and holistic education to help all individuals strengthen their sense of bondedness with the universe. We value our connections with one another and the world because it is through such connections that we are invited into compassion.

Compassion

Throughout our liberal religious history, we have been blessed with women and men whose compassion and courage provide examples for us all. We learn about heroines and heroes such as Dorothea Dix, Clara Barton, Horace Mann, and James Reeb in our lifespan religious education classes. We recognize that their struggles are with us today in different forms. We are reminded by their work that, if we do not feel compassion, we may well stunt our lives and threaten the future of our planet.

In all of our religious education programming—be it church school, youth groups, intergenerational events, or adult education—we offer as a ground rule for all our activities the acceptance of one another and the valuing of our inherent worth and dignity as persons. We acknowledge that there is evil, pain, and suffering in the world. We do not close our eyes to any of this. We commit ourselves to trying to understand how to help individuals and groups untie knots of pain and anger. We commit ourselves to stand with one another through the joys and sorrows that affect every life.

We often encourage our church school classes to include social action as part of their educational process. One seventh- and eighth-grade class in a Philadelphia congregation focused their efforts on the need to care for the earth by recycling paper. They learned about church governance when they convinced the board of the church to vote in favor of a recycling proposal which called for the use of more white than colored paper in any printing done by the church. They persuaded the adults to put out bins so that parishioners could recycle their Sunday programs when they were finished with them.

In our religious education programs, we also try to find ways to support and encourage the work of many heroic individuals in our congregations who quietly go about the hard work of trying to make the world a better place every day. When a church member in Virginia retired from his lifetime work as the owner and chief chef of a diner, for example, he began working five days a week as the breakfast cook for a local homeless program. He still rose at 4 A.M., but his destination was very different. I remember the response of the church school children who heard him tell his story. He was not boasting. He was glad to be of help and merely shared in honesty the challenges he faced in serving the homeless. In the next few weeks, the children mounted a drive to bring to the congregation's attention the need for more food for the shelter. The result was an outpouring of gifts, a testament to "com-passion"—that is, passion with and for the struggles of others.

Offering compassion is difficult when there are as many demands upon us as there are today. Our religious education programs engage us in the act of compassion: the offering of a helping hand, walking together for a cause, the solidarity felt in a community social action project. It is such engagement which can rekindle our spirits in important ways. And it is this spirit which inspires the third component of liberal religious education: creativity.

Creativity

With Channing's call to us in 1837 to "touch inward springs," the seed of creativity was planted in the ground of liberal religious education. It took decades before it bore fruit. And yet, with each evolutionary turn of Unitarian and Universalist religious education, more and more emphasis has been placed on this important foundation of the liberal religious quest. Gabriel Moran, a noted liberal religious educator, expresses it eloquently when he says that "religious education is the attempt to keep education open to the undreamt-of possibilities of the human race."

I am very aware of the changes that take place as our children move from the wide-eyed, wonderful imagination of young childhood into a more closed and limited mode of engagement with the world, as schools and society try to define for us what is and what is not real, actual, or possible. Our Unitarian Universalist religious education programs are places where dreams may be kindled or rekindled, where wondering and imagination can be affirmed, where new talents can be tried in safe settings. An adult class in religious dance, a course in poetry writing, a workshop in art for the non-artistic can open doors for people, no matter what their age. Intergenerational events when all ages try their talents at something new are especially rich times for growth. Non-competitive games can open doors to new fun for those who have not felt especially gifted athletically. An afternoon kite-making and kite-flying event *can* help spirits soar.

The challenges facing each of us can best be met when our creative potential is open and flowing. The more affirmed a person feels in using his or her own individual creative gifts, the more likely she or he will be able to handle a situation with a sense of connection, compassion, and maturity. The more frustrated the inner flame of being, the more likely a person is to respond in blocked, prejudiced, and limited ways.

Connections, compassion, and creativity are the gifts of lifespan liberal religious education. Ours is a tradition which has long nurtured such values. Ours is a tradition which is open to continuing growth and new learnings in these areas. Ours is a tradition which invites every individual to be an integral part of the creation of such religious education programs, activities, and events. In such ways, we further our vision of a responsive and responsible religious community.

Makanah Elizabeth Morriss

Our Action for Social Justice

One does not need to probe too deeply into the life of a Unitarian Universalist congregation to discover evidence of how committed individual Unitarian Universalists are to social justice. These commitments run deep.

I think of the Unitarian Universalist woman who carefully washed all her plastic bags from the supermarket, hanging them up with clothespins on a line over her sink. I think of the man who ran for public office on an environmental platform, knowing he would lose but dedicating his personal resources to the campaign anyway. Another woman, a grandmother, never missed the opportunity to testify against anti-choice or anti-gay rights legislation that surfaced with menacing frequency.

When I served as a parish minister, I was an active member of the state women's lobby. For me, social justice activism found its most compelling commitment in the women's movement. As a Unitarian Universalist, I had lots of company. But even those in my congregation who did not share my commitment to feminist political action supported my right to use my energies in that arena. As individuals, we Unitarian Universalists reckon with the questions of how to act on our faith. What matters most is that our actions are congruent with what we believe.

A Unitarian Universalist congregation offers individuals a network of opportunities to become involved with social justice issues. Many individuals join a Unitarian Universalist congregation precisely for that reason. But some people prefer to keep their political and their spiritual lives separate, and that is why most Unitarian Universalist congregations present a diverse set of programs for service and for witness. We try to respect the fact that each person's approach to social action is different. No one is required to be involved in social action in order to be a part of a congregation's life.

Congregational Social Action

The issue of a corporate social justice commitment is somewhat more complex. It is rooted in our democratic process. Sometimes a congregation may vote to take a corporate position on an important public issue. The stands a congregation may take derive their authority from the accepted democratic process that is the center of our religious life.

Our Unitarian Universalist faith expresses itself in the form of religious democracy in which the process of governance and decision-making is as important as the outcome. Ministers and leadership are elected, budgets voted, and all issues of concern to the community are debated in open meetings. Each person's opinion is not only respected—it is protected. And the integrity of the community is judged according to its ability to honor the viewpoints of diverse individuals while achieving institutional effectiveness. It's a delicate balance, but the dynamic tension between individualism and community that has shaped our religious tradition is also the vehicle for the expression of social justice values.

One of the disciplines of social action in a Unitarian Universalist community is the concern for right relation: the balance of power and freedom among individuals as they are related in community. Democratic process ensures justice in relationships while preserving individual freedom at the same time. Our vision of the just community—imperfectly realized, but embraced all the same—is of an environment in which freedom, tolerance, and mutual respect nurture individual empowerment and help people become effective agents for justice in the world.

These values have, throughout our history, illuminated the injustices both inside and outside our own religious community. Unitarians and Universalists have exercised significant leadership, in Europe and in North America, in the causes of religious freedom, women's suffrage, abolition of slavery, civil rights, and reproductive self-determination. At the same time, we have evolved in the way we look at ourselves and our own norms and privileges. In recent years we have struggled to correct our institution and to achieve right relation with one another as we learn how to make our community sensitive and welcoming to women's experiences and realities, to lesbian and gay persons, to differently abled people, and to a new understanding of human difference.

The concern for social justice, then, is embedded in community life as well as in individual empowerment. Our ability to address social issues in a corporate fashion is only as good as our ability to preserve justice in our own religious community. Individuals find support for their social justice commitments to the extent that they find support for who they are as persons.

Resolutions of Social Justice

Nevertheless, Unitarian Universalists seek opportunities to speak with one voice on the social issues of the day. One opportunity is the General Resolutions process by which the Unitarian Universalist Association (UUA) gains the authority to advocate on behalf of our membership. Each year, the annual meeting of Unitarian Universalist congregations (the General Assembly) votes resolutions on current social issues. Local congregations or districts initiate these resolutions, which are reviewed by the UUA Commission on General Resolutions and then submitted to all congregations in a "parish poll." The three resolutions that receive the highest number of affirmative votes from the parish poll are placed on the General Assembly agenda.

In the first year a resolution appears on the General Assembly agenda, the Assembly only decides whether or not to refer that resolution to congregations for a year's worth of study. The Department for Social Justice prepares study guides to the resolutions, exploring background and presenting balanced arguments concerning the issues. The Commission seeks feedback from congregations studying the resolutions. After a year's study, the proposed guidelines (now amended in accord with the responses from congregations) go before the Assembly again for final action.

The General Resolutions enable the Unitarian Universalist community to use a collective voice in social justice debate. The resolutions are created and refined through democratic process. They do not pretend to represent the views of every Unitarian Universalist, and individuals are free to disagree with them. But as the UUA President, the Moderator, the Board, and the staff of the Social Justice Department encounter public issues and give witness to Unitarian Universalist values, the resolutions provide both guidelines and support to their actions.

Becoming Effective Agents of Change

UUA public witness through the General Resolutions is only

one way our religious institutions attempt to nurture social action. Recognizing that the nature of social change is local and personal, inseparable from the communities in which people actually live, Unitarian Universalists have turned increasing amounts of attention and institutional resources to training for empowerment in local social action. The UUA Department for Social Justice supports a network of district trainers who work with local congregations, helping them to learn the skills to be effective social change agents in their own communities.

UUA support for training is another expression of the democratic process in our religious community. While some social justice issues are urgently global, others are supremely local. Canadian and US congregations have different social agendas. Individuals vary within individual congregations, and all need the tools to act on their commitments. The training network that has emerged in recent years responds to the need to equip individuals with the tools they can use in their own local context. In this way, individual commitment is supported and sustained by the discerning use of collective power.

Similarly, the UUA supports a variety of emerging and active social justice groups that form around pressing contemporary issues. At this writing, Unitarian Universalist interest groups include those focusing on the environment, the increasing violence against women, a just economic community, men's issues, and racial justice. In addition, the UUA belongs to several interfaith coalitions, including Project Equality (which monitors equal employment opportunities in business) and the Interfaith Center for Corporate Responsibility (which promotes socially responsible investing).

Making Our Own Community Just

The Unitarian Universalist commitment to social justice cannot be separated from our own self-assessment as to whether or not we are a just democratic community. Thus, many of our most compelling public social justice commitments have begun as internal dialogues only to become prophetic leadership to the religious community and in the rest of society. Three examples of this process involve women's issues, lesbian and gay concerns, and racial and cultural diversity.

Women and Religion

In 1977, the General Assembly passed the Women and Religion Resolution. The text reads, in part, "Therefore be it resolved: That the 1977 General Assembly calls upon all Unitarian Universalists to examine carefully their own religious beliefs and the extent to which these beliefs influence sex-role stereotypes within their own families . . . [and] requests the Unitarian Universalist Association to join with those who are encouraging others in the society to examine the relationship between religious and cultural attitudes toward women. . . ." (The full text of the resolution can be found in the *Resolutions and Resources Handbook*.)

One outcome of this resolution was the formation of the Women and Religion Committee, the Association's agency to promote social justice for women *within* our own community. The Women and Religion Committee has worked since 1977 to further the objectives of the resolution and to influence the UUA response to women's issues. At the same time, the Unitarian Universalist Women's Federation (see the listing at the end of this essay) began to address itself more directly to issues of concern to contemporary women. Both groups, working together and separately, have effected change for our movement. Awareness of women's issues and interest in the religious implications of feminism have informed our programming, governance, and leadership ever since.

Lesbian and Gay Concerns

The first General Resolution calling for end to discrimination against homosexuals and bisexuals was voted in 1970, out of the recognition that there are Unitarian Universalists who are gay, lesbian, and bisexual; that discrimination exists against gay, lesbian, and bisexual people; and that homosexuality is a normal expression of human sexual orientation. Since that first resolution, many important steps have been taken. The Association has established an Office of Lesbian and Gay Concerns; a non-discrimination clause in our bylaws ensures fair employment practices in ministerial settlement for gays, lesbians, and bisexuals; the General Assembly has affirmed those ministers who provide services of union for gay and lesbian couples; and the UUA has developed the Welcoming Congregation program to encourage congregations to make gays, lesbians, and bisexuals feel welcome in our societies.

Racial and Cultural Diversity

Unitarian Universalists have called for racial justice ever since the first UUA General Assembly in 1961. But as a religious community we have also fallen short of making real the inclusiveness we affirm in principle. At times we have been troubled by our struggle to reach consensus about the means by which we can achieve our goal of a just, diverse, and enriched religious community. Lately there is reason to hope that we may realize our vision at last.

The 1992 General Assembly voted a Resolution of Immediate Witness, "Racial and Cultural Diversity in Unitarian Universalism," that resolved to affirm and support this vision of a racially diverse and multicultural Unitarian Universalism. This exciting new initiative is described in more detail in the essay called "Our Commitment to Racial and Cultural Diversity," included in this *Pocket Guide*.

These are examples of ways in which consciousness-raising inside our community is made manifest in action. They are "works in progress" which change as we adapt to new insights and revised consensus. They are evidence that democratic process can move from the individual to the collective and from the personal to the political.

Other Agencies of Social Change

The Unitarian Universalist community includes several different agencies, beyond the UUA and its departments, that address social justice concerns. They meet together as a coalition, the Social Action Clearing House (SACH), which plans events at the General Assembly and participates in an annual Washington, DC, training and lobbying session. While the representation on SACH varies, the following organizations belong to SACH and are also Associate Member Organizations of the UUA.

Unitarian Universalist Service Committee

Since 1939, the Unitarian Universalist Service Committee (UUSC) has been working to create a more just and humane world. By supporting programs around the world that improve education, health care, food production, job skills, and human rights, the UUSC enables people to help themselves. In the United States, the UUSC educates citizens and advocates for international policies by promoting mutual respect and independence. Its children's program focuses on improving the lives and well-being of children in the United States. The UUSC's bylaws specify four approaches aimed at eradicating the root causes of injustice: provide experiences that promote freedom and self-determination, resist and change oppressive institutions and practices, educate and mobilize individuals and groups for service and action, and provide emergency relief. *Unitarian Universalist Service Committee, 130 Prospect Street, Cambridge, MA 02139.*

Unitarian Universalist United Nations Office

The Unitarian Universalist United Nations Office (UU-UNO) is the major channel for the UUA to influence world affairs and the United Nations. The UU-UNO has two functions. First, its staff and volunteers represent the UUA and the International Association for Religious Freedom at UN Headquarters. Through daily contact with delegates and UN staff members, the UU-UNO works with like-minded organizations to monitor and support UN work in disarmament, human rights, and environmental protection. Second, the UU-UNO informs and mobilizes Unitarian Universalists across the continent, keeping them aware of the United Nations and showing how they can help the United Nations be more effective. *Unitarian Universalist United Nations Office, 777 UN Plaza, Suite 7D, New York, NY 10017.*

Unitarian Universalist Women's Federation

The mission of the Unitarian Universalist Women's Federation (UUWF) is "to enable Unitarian Universalist women to join together for mutual support, personal growth, and spiritual enrichment and, through their combined strength and vision, to work toward a future where all women will be empowered to live their lives with a sense of wholeness and integrity in a world at peace that recognizes the worth and dignity of each individual." The Federation is an organization of 6,000 women and men who join either as individuals or as groups in local churches. It was formed in 1963 by a consolidation of Unitarian and Universalist women's organizations. *Unitarian Universalist Women's Federation, 25 Beacon Street, Boston, MA 02108.*

Judith E. Meyer

Our Commitment to Racial and Cultural Diversity

Growing up in the 1940s and 50s was an experience filled with remarkable contradictions and transitions. Segregation was the law in many states of the land, and people of color were denied the full rights and benefits of citizenship. In spite of that, my family experience was one of multiculturalism and class inclusiveness.

I was born and raised in Columbus, OH. I am a product of African-American, Native-American, and European-American heritages and was brought up to appreciate and respect the history and contributions of each of these cultures. In other words, I did not see the world strictly in terms of black and white.

My immediate family included my parents and my brother. My extended family included my grandparents and several aunts, uncles, and cousins who all lived nearby. We cousins formed a network that made us as close as brothers and sisters. Birthdays and holidays were opportunities for our rainbow family to come together, appreciate one another, and share our love. This experience helped shape my view of what a family looks and acts like.

Ours was a working-class neighborhood that was primarily, though not exclusively, black. I went to a segregated elementary school which, ironically, worked ultimately to my advantage. Our African-American teachers and principal were highly educated and motivated. They were great role models. They believed in us, expected us to learn, and taught us the lessons of surviving in a segregated society while also instilling in us the vision of a new, integrated world. My junior high school was integrated—on both the student and faculty levels. Just prior to my high school years, we moved from our primarily black neighborhood on the east side of Columbus to a predominantly white neighborhood on the west side, where I attended an overwhelmingly white high school and was a "minority" for the first time.

A Complex Religious Journey

As an Episcopalian, I encountered segregation in the church. I was a member of a predominantly black congregation that welcomed whites at a time when blacks were not welcomed by our white counterpart congregations. Many members of my congregation were economically upwardly mobile and were "come-outers" from traditional black churches. Our membership included many of the best minds and most successful business and professional members of the black community. Although neither of my parents was a college graduate, their intellect was respected and they held positions of leadership in the church. Our congregation valued the rational search for truth and allowed for theological and cultural differences.

Although my mother was director of religious education, I challenged many of the Sunday school teachings and concepts of Christianity, including the Trinity. Even so, I was still accepted as a member of that community and was encouraged to seek leadership roles for myself. Yet as I participated in the civil rights movement during my college career at Ohio State University and confronted the role of mainline Christianity in maintaining racism, I found myself less comfortable with my Episcopal roots. Later, I was to find the social activism of Unitarian Universalism appealing for its confrontation with segregation and its opposition to the Vietnam War and support for women's rights.

I entered seminary in Rochester, NY, unsure of how or if I could authentically live out my personal beliefs and be a traditional Christian minister. I was impressed with the ministries of the Unitarian Universalist congregations in Rochester and began to consider a relationship with Unitarian Universalism. Yet, having been initially encouraged by Unitarian Universalism's pioneering response to black self-empowerment in the late 1960s, I became disillusioned as the denomination's commitments seemed to unravel in the early 1970s. Disappointed, I turned to the ecumenical movement. Still, I was frustrated not to have a faith to call my own.

I had met my wife, Rose Edington, during my seminary years. We were a study in contrasts: male/female; urban/rural; Episcopalian/Baptist; black/white. We both became ministers but were uncomfortable with the religions of our childhood. When our daughter, Melanie, was born, she was, of course, a multiracial, multicultural and multireligious child. We wanted for her what we had experienced growing up—a religious community that nurtured her self-esteem and a faith that exposed her to values of justice, equity, and peace—but we were not sure it would be possible to find. This led me to reconsider Unitarian Universalism. I decided that joining our local Unitarian Universalist society was the best choice for our family.

The African-American Experience and Unitarian Universalism

African-Americans have been involved with Unitarianism and Universalism from the earliest days of those faiths in America. Gloster Dalton, a former slave, was one of the twelve founding members of the first Universalist church, the Independent Christian Church of Gloucester, MA. Both free men and women and escapees from slavery are recorded as attending Unitarian congregations in the Boston and Philadelphia areas.

Unitarians and Universalists were found on both sides of the slavery issue. Those who favored abolition advocated a wide variety of strategies from nonviolent resistance to proactive efforts. Universalists such as Benjamin Rush, president of the Pennsylvania Society for Promoting the Abolition of Slavery, were among the first persons to call for an end to that "peculiar institution." Many Universalists found slavery inconsistent with their belief that all God's children are part of the same family.

A number of Unitarians were followers of William Lloyd Garrison, editor of *The Liberator*, the leading anti-slavery newspaper, and himself a Unitarian. Among them were Samuel May, Lydia Maria Child, William Ellery Channing, and Theodore Parker. One of the classic stories of those times is that of the Rev. Theodore Parker, who provided sanctuary for several blacks in his church. A noted preacher, Parker always kept a loaded pistol on the pulpit and publicly declared that he would shoot anyone who tried to remove blacks from his congregation.

One prominent African-American Unitarian of this era was Frances Ellen Watkins Harper. Born in Baltimore in 1825, she lived in Philadelphia most of her adult life. Poet, novelist, essayist, she was a tireless abolitionist, stalwart supporter of the underground railroad; and dedicated advocate for women's rights. So gifted at public speaking, she was considered on a par with Frederick Douglass. She was a member of First Unitarian Church of Philadelphia and worked with the African Methodist Episcopal denomination on developing their religious education curriculum.

Not only were Unitarian Universalists important in the abolitionist movement and instrumental in the success of the underground railroad, but they were also among the first to call for education and health care for freed slaves. After Reconstruction, as the country became resegregated under Jim Crow laws, Unitarians and Universalists were leaders in the fight to defeat discriminatory laws and promote equal rights for all people. They introduced legislation within the political arena and actively supported court decisions that promoted equality and justice.

The 1960s produced many leaders, among them Whitney M. Young, Jr., an active Unitarian Universalist. As the Executive Director of the National Urban League from 1961 to 1971, Young brought the League into the civil rights movement and made it a force in the major events and debates of that tumultuous decade. He was also a leader of the 1963 March on Washington. Young's work helped bring about historic breakthroughs for people of color in employment, education, and entrepreneurship. He was the author of two books, *To Be Equal* and *Beyond Racism*, through which he developed his vision of an open society. What he envisioned was a pluralistic society—not simply an integrated one—that would thrive on ethnic and cultural diversity and ensure economic and racial justice.

But Young's was not the only leadership Unitarian Universalism provided the civil rights movement. Viola Liuzzo, a homemaker and lay member of First Unitarian Church of Detroit, was brutally murdered for serving as a driver for voter registration efforts in the South. The Rev. James Reeb, like hundreds of other clergy, had responded to Martin Luther King, Jr.'s call to participate in the first march on Selma, AL, in March of 1965. After the march, he and two other Unitarian Universalist ministers were attacked by whites as they were walking back to their rooms after dining at a black restaurant. Jim was struck on the back of the head and killed. The UUA Board of Trustees, upon hearing of Jim's death, adjourned its meeting in Boston and reconvened in Selma, where Board members and half the ministers in the Association participated in a successful march.

After Selma, Unitarian Universalists throughout the country stepped up their efforts to open closed doors that denied basic human rights to African-Americans. The Association was among the first predominantly white religious organizations to respond positively to the new directions of the black empowerment movement in the late 1960s.

Right Commitment, Inadequate Response

One of the strengths of Unitarian Universalism is its belief that speaking the truth is essential for authentic spiritual growth, individual development, and institutional change. Although progressive in dealing with racism within society, Unitarian Universalism has been slower to address it internally. Until the 1980s there were only a handful of African-Americans in parish ministry or denominational leadership positions. Too often in the past, issues of race and class within the Association hindered the development of black religious professionals and the creation of appropriate resources to speak to and serve African-American needs.

The first major history of black ministers' experiences within Unitarian Universalism, *Black Pioneers in a White Denomination,* was produced in 1980 by the Rev. Mark Morrison-Reed. In his book, Mark states, "The quandary I face is twofold. First, given my chosen vocation as a minister in a white denomination, how can I serve the black community? And, second, how can I inform the Unitarian Universalist tradition through the black experience?" Mark lifts up a reality that most African-Americans experience in Unitarian Universalism: the sense of living in two worlds. The challenge historically has been to find a common ground in which our heritage and our faith can find congruence.

Historically, Unitarian Universalists have been on the cutting edge of social justice advocacy, but many have been ill-prepared to recognize and acknowledge institutional racism within Unitarian Universalism. In the 1960s, black civil rights activists in the pursuit of racial justice aggressively confronted the UUA. They sought more power and participation, the establishment of a Black Affairs Council, and a greater voice for African-Americans in the Association's decision-making and operations. It was during this era that Unitarian Universalism had a significant increase in its African-American membership.

The 1968 General Assembly, after much debate and controversy, voted to create the Black Affairs Council (BAC). Despite strong commitment by some individuals and congregations, suspicion, misunderstanding, and lack of funds contributed to the ultimate demise of BAC. The majority of white Unitarian Universalists did not accept the responsibility to understand and nurture the program they had dared to embrace in 1968. In spite of the dismay of many, this lack of support for the program became a source of division between those persons committed to cultural assimilation and those who advocated self-empowerment. Events came to a head at the 1969 General Assembly in Boston, and in 1970 funding for the BAC was eliminated. These actions resulted for some people in feelings of disenfranchisement and, unfortunately, in the eventual departure of a significant number of African-

American as well as white Unitarian Universalists. What has become clear, in retrospect, is that our painful experiences were once again those of pioneers. We confronted new problems of race before other religious groups did. How could we have known at the time that the model of racial assimilation and integration for which we had fought so long was inadequate to address the newly felt needs for empowerment?

During the 1970s Unitarian Universalists were very active in opposing the Vietnam War and in fighting for women's and gay and lesbian rights, all of which was positive, but the issue of race was put on the back burner. This lack of focus hindered the development of effective programs and initiatives for African-Americans and other people of color at the very time, ironically, when the number of people of color who were open to liberal agendas was increasing.

Learning from Our Past

It took us nearly a decade to heal our wounds from the black empowerment controversy—to acknowledge our mistakes, renew our commitment, and sharpen our understanding about the "new racism" of the 1980s. In 1981, recognizing the need to look again at racism within the Association, the UUA Board of Trustees contracted with Community Change, Inc. of Boston for an institutional racism audit. This audit dealt with issues of race at UUA headquarters. The Board adopted the following anti-racism imperative in 1981 and reaffirmed it in 1989:

> Recognizing the fact that institutional racism is still embedded in American society in 1981, the Unitarian Universalist Association shall seek to eliminate racism in all its institutional structures, policies, practices, and patterns of behavior so that it will become a racially equitable institution and can make an effec-

tive contribution toward achieving a similarly equitable society.

Recognizing that words alone weren't enough, a series of task forces for monitoring racism were established in the 1980s. The Association helped found several intentionally multiracial congregations with persons of color in leadership. In 1983, the Network of Black Unitarian Universalists was formed, and in 1985 a General Assembly resolution established the Black Concerns Working Group (BCWG) to work with congregations and Unitarian Universalist organizations seeking to counteract racism. An intentional affirmative action effort was launched.

A new staff position at the UUA was created in 1987 to focus on racial and urban concerns. In 1988, the African-American Unitarian Universalist Ministry (AAUUM) was formed as a continental organization for African-American ministers and religious professionals. In 1989, the Office of Racial Inclusiveness was established.

A New Commitment, A Right Response

A series of meetings from 1990 to 1992 laid the groundwork for developing a long-range initiative for racial and cultural diversity. At the 1992 General Assembly, a resolution called "Racial and Cultural Diversity in Unitarian Universalism" was passed. The significance of this experience is captured by the insightful words of the Rev. Victor Carpenter, the maker of the motion:

> We have been provided with that rarest of human opportunities—a second chance. Twenty-five years ago we had the opportunity to lead this country's religious community in the direction of racial justice.

> We rose up and we fell back. The vision was too blurred, the rhetoric too harsh, the pain too deep. Now we are again given a chance to lead this nation in generous response to the social crisis symbolized by [the] Los Angeles [civil disturbances]. We are called to do justly, to love mercy, and to work humbly for the empowerment of our brothers and sisters. Let's not blow it.

This time we didn't blow it; in fact we did something rare for Unitarian Universalists: we passed the resolution unanimously! Once again we are on the cutting edge in terms of racism, race relations, and religion.

The world is undergoing radical changes demographically and geographically. Old boundaries and relationships are breaking down and new ones are emerging. As we prepare to enter a new century, we have a faith that places a high value on a person's freedom to choose, to question authority, to pursue truth wherever it is found, to respect the worth and dignity of all people. We are committed to justice, peace, equity, right relationships, and the preservation of a sustainable universe. North America currently has the highest number of middle and upper income, highly educated, socially conscious people of color in its history—not just African-American but Latinos, Asians, and many others. They are pioneering new paths professionally, socially, and spiritually. Our faith speaks to the conditions of our time and is an option that needs to be made known to these pioneers.

The world needs a new paradigm of racial cooperation and partnership. Unitarian Universalism is working to be an anti-racist multicultural faith that incorporates the talents and gifts of people of color at all levels. Our desire is to truly honor the history, experiences, insights, and culture of people of color and to live our faith together as we create a humane, anti-racist, multicultural world. To remain socially relevant and to prepare our children and grandchildren for the world they will live in, Unitarian Universalism needs people of color as members. People of color who are progressive, open to new insights and experiences, and committed to authentic multicultural relationships can address society's ills with a faith like ours. We are convinced that together we can create a new world.

Melvin A. Hoover

Important Dates in Unitarian Universalist History

Early Christian History

225 Origen, one of the church Fathers, writes *On First Principles*, advocating belief in universal salvation.

325 Nicene Creed adopted at Council of Nicaea establishes dogma of the Trinity.

544 Belief in universal salvation condemned as heresy by a church council.

The Reformation

1511 Birth of Michael Servetus (the most famous of the sixteenth-century anti-Trinitarians).

1527 Martin Cellarius publishes *On the Works of God* (the earliest anti-Trinitarian book).

1531 Michael Servetus publishes *On the Errors of the Trinity*.

1553 Michael Servetus is burned at the stake in Geneva.

Polish Socinianism

1539 Birth of Faustus Socinus (leader of the Polish Socinian, or Polish Brethren, movement).

1546 Anti-Trinitarianism appears in Poland.

1579 Faustus Socinus arrives in Poland.

1585 Founding of the Rakow press (the first official Unitarian press).

1591 The Socinian Church in Krakow is destroyed by a mob.

1658 The Polish Diet banishes Socinians.

Transylvanian (Hungarian) Unitarianism

1510 Birth of Francis David (leader of Transylvanian Unitarians).

1566 Francis David preaches against the doctrine of the Trinity.

1568 King John Sigismund (the Unitarian King) proclaims the earliest edict of complete religious toleration.

1579 Francis David, condemned as a heretic, dies in prison.

1821 English and Transylvanian Unitarians discover one another.

English Unitarianism and Universalism

1550 The Church of the Strangers is established in London.

1615 Birth of John Biddle (the founder of English Unitarianism).

1654 John Biddle is banished to the Scilly Isles.

1703 Thomas Emlyn is imprisoned at Dublin for anti-Trinitarian beliefs.

Birth of George de Benneville (one of the leaders of American Universalism) in London.

1723 Birth of Theophilus Lindsey (one of the founders of the English Unitarian movement).

1733 Birth of Joseph Priestley (one of the greatest scientists of his age, the discoverer of oxygen, and a founder of both the English and American Unitarian movements).

1741 John Murray (the founder of American Universalism) born in Alton, England.

George de Benneville immigrates to Pennsylvania.

1750 James Relly, an associate of the evangelist George Whitefield, withdraws from this connection and establishes himself as an independent preacher of Universalism.

1759 *Union* (a theological treatise on universal salvation) by James Relly published in London.

1774 Essex Street Chapel opened in London (marking the beginning of permanently organized Unitarianism in England).

1791 Riots against Joseph Priestley and other Unitarians in Birmingham.

1794 Joseph Priestley immigrates to America.

1825 The British and Foreign Unitarian Association founded.

Canadian Unitarianism and Universalism

1832 First recorded meeting of Unitarians in Montreal.

1842 First permanent Unitarian church established in Montreal.

1843 A Universalist church established in Halifax.

1845 First Unitarian Church of Toronto established.

1891 An Icelandic-speaking Unitarian Church organized in Winnipeg. (Between 1891 and 1931, other Icelandic-speaking Unitarian Churches organized.)

1961 Canadian Unitarian Council organized.

1962 Canadian Unitarian Council/Conseil Unitaire Canadien relates itself officially to the UUA.

American Unitarianism and Universalism

1637 Samuel Gorton (a pioneer of Christian Universalism) driven out of Massachusetts for his political and religious radicalism.

1684 Joseph Gatchell has his tongue pierced with a red-hot iron for his statement, "All men should be saved."

1740 High point of the Great Awakening (whose emotional excesses stimulated a desire for a more rational religion).

1743 Christopher Sower (a Universalist Quaker) with the assistance of George de Benneville, prints the first Bible in America translated into German. Passages supporting the universal character of religion were printed in heavier type.

1770 John Murray arrives at Good Luck Point on Barnegat Bay, NJ.

On September 30, Murray preaches his first sermon in America in the meetinghouse of Thomas Potter.

1771 Birth of Universalist Hosea Ballou, in Richmond, NH.

1774 John Murray preaches in Gloucester, MA.

1778 Caleb Rich organizes the General Society (Universalist) to ordain ministers and issue preaching licenses.

1779 Gloucester Universalists organize the first Universalist church in America and call John Murray as minister.

1785 Liturgy of King's Chapel Boston, is revised, omitting references to the Trinity.

The first Universalist Convention (with delegates from churches) held in Oxford, MA.

1786 Gloucester Universalists successfully contest the right of the state to raise taxes for the established church.

A Universalist church (called the Universal Baptist Church) organized in Philadelphia.

1787 Congregation of King's Chapel, disregarding Episcopal procedures, ordains lay reader James Freeman as its minister, thereby becoming the first independent church of Unitarian beliefs.

1788 Murray wins the right of Universalists and dissenting ministers to be recognized as ordained ministers with authority to perform marriages.

1790 The Philadelphia Convention of Universalists adopts a declaration of faith and a set of principles of social reform.

1793 Second Universalist Convention in Oxford, MA, marks founding of precursor of Universalist Church in America.

1796 Joseph Priestley advocates Universalism and Unitarianism in Philadelphia. Founding of the First Unitarian Church of Philadelphia with encouragement of Priestley.

1802 The oldest Pilgrim church in America (founded at Plymouth in 1620) becomes Unitarian.

1803 Winchester Profession of Faith adopted by Universalists at Winchester, NH.

1805 Hosea Ballou writes *A Treatise on Atonement* (the first book published in America openly rejecting the doctrine of the Trinity).

Election of Henry Ware to Hollis Professor of Divinity at Harvard College begins Unitarian controversy.

1811 Harvard Divinity School established.

Maria Cook preaches first sermon by a woman in a Universalist pulpit.

1819 William Ellery Channing delivers his Baltimore sermon (a landmark statement of Unitarian principles).

The Christian Leader (Universalist) begins publication (originally named *The Universalist Magazine*).

1821 *The Christian Register* (Unitarian) begins publication.

1825 The American Unitarian Association is organized.

1833 Formation of The General Convention of Universalists in the United States (with advisory powers only).

1836 Publication of first major Transcendentalist works.

1838 Ralph Waldo Emerson delivers "The Divinity School Address" (a major event in religious liberalism).

1840 Brook Farm founded by the Ripleys.

1841 Theodore Parker delivers his South Boston sermon "The Transient and Permanent in Christianity" (in defense of natural religion).

Adin Ballou founds Hopedale Community.

1844 Meadville Theological School established in Meadville, PA.

1846 Adin Ballou's book, *Christian Non-Resistance,* advocating nonviolence, influences Tolstoy.

1847 The Universalist General Reform Association is organized.

1852 Tufts College founded by Universalists at Medford, MA.

1854 Publication of the first book under American Unitarian Association imprint—*Grains of God, or Select Thoughts on Sacred Themes* by the Rev. Cyrus A. Bartol, Jr.

1856 St. Lawrence University and Theological School founded by Universalists at Canton, NY.

1862 The Universalist Publishing House established.

1863 Ordination of Olympia Brown, arguably the first woman to be ordained by any denomination.

1865 The National Conference of Unitarian Churches organized.

1866 Organization of the Universalist General Convention (renamed in 1942 the Universalist Church of America).

1867 The Free Religious Association is organized.

1869 Women's Centenary Association formed (in 1939 became the Association of Universalist Women).

1880 The General Alliance of Unitarian and Other Liberal Christian Women (originally called Women's Auxiliary Conference) is organized.

1884 The American Unitarian Association becomes an association representative of and directly responsible to its member churches.

1889 Young People's Christian Union formed (later called Universalist Youth Fellowship).

Joseph Jordan ordained as first African-American Universalist minister.

1890 Universalists establish churches in Japan.

1896 Unitarian Young People's Religious Union organized.

1899 "Essential Principles of Universalism" adopted in Boston, MA.

First Merger Commission founded.

1900 The International Congress of Free Christians and Other Religious Liberals (today the International Association for Religious Freedom), the oldest international interfaith body, formed.

1902 Beacon Press launched (broadening the American Unitarian Association's publishing program) with *Some Ethical Phases of the Labor Question*, by Carroll Wright.

1904 Starr King School for the Ministry founded in Berkeley, CA, as Pacific Unitarian School of the Ministry.

1908 The Unitarian Fellowship for Social Justice organized.

1913 The General Sunday School Association organized at Utica, NY.

1917 The first denomination-wide Unitarian Youth Sunday held.

Universalist General Convention adopts "Declaration of Social Principles" written by Clarence Skinner.

1920 The Unitarian Laymen's League organized.

1921 Universalist women acquire Clara Barton homestead (developed into camp for diabetic girls).

1931 Second Merger Commission.

1933 Free Church of America formed.

1934 Commission on Appraisal appointed by American Unitarian Association.

1935 Washington Statement of Faith adopted by Universalists.

1936 AUA Commission on Appraisal publishes *Unitarians Face a New Age.*

1937 The Unitarian Sunday School Society merged with the Religious Education Department of the American Unitarian Association.

Frederick May Eliot elected president of the AUA; Sophia Lyon Fahs appointed Children's Editor.

1938 The Beacon Press pioneers a series of publications in religious education.

1939 Unitarian Service Committee organized.

1941 Young People's Christian Union reorganized into Universalist Youth Fellowship.

1942 The Young People's Religious Union reorganized into American Unitarian Youth.

The Universalist General Convention renamed the Universalist Church of America.

1943 The Unitarian Service Committee makes plans for medical missions to war-devastated countries.

1944 The Church of the Larger Fellowship organized to serve Unitarians living in areas without Unitarian churches.

1945 The Universalist Service Committee formed.

1948 Continental program to establish Unitarian fellowships begun.

1949 Charles Street Meeting House, Boston, MA, initiated by American Universalists.

1950 American and English Unitarians jointly celebrate the 125th anniversary of their respective denominational organizations.

1953 Liberal Religious Youth, Inc., is formed by the merger of American Unitarian Youth and Universalist Youth Fellowship.

The Council of Liberal Churches (Universalist-Unitarian), Inc., is organized for the federation of the departments of publications, education, and public relations.

The Christian Leader renamed the *Universalist Leader*.

1956 Unitarians and Universalists create Joint Commission on Merger to examine feasibility of merging the two denominations.

1958 *The Christian Register* renamed *The Unitarian Register.*

1961 The American Unitarian Association and the Universalist Church of America officially consolidate and organize the Unitarian Universalist Association.

The Unitarian Register and *The Universalist Leader* are merged as the Unitarian Universalist *Register-Leader.*

1962 The Unitarian Laymen's League and the National Association of Universalist Men join to form the Laymen's League (Unitarian-Universalist).

1963 The Alliance of Unitarian Women and the Association of Universalist Women join to form the Unitarian Universalist Women's Federation.

The Unitarian Service Committee and the Department of World Service of the Unitarian Universalist Association unite to form the Unitarian Universalist Service Committee, Inc.

First General Assembly resolution in support of abortion rights.

1964 First resolution against the Vietnam War passed by a General Assembly.

1965 James Reeb, Unitarian Universalist minister, murdered in Selma, AL, in civil rights protest organized by Martin Luther King, Jr. As a result, protest intensifies across the nation. UUA Board adjourns in the middle of its meeting and moves meeting site to Selma.

1966 Martin Luther King, Jr., delivers Ware Lecture at General Assembly.

1967 Black Unitarian Universalist Caucus organized.

1970 *Unitarian Universalist World* succeeds *Register-Leader*.

1971 *About Your Sexuality* curriculum for junior high youth published.

1972 Beacon Press publishes *Pentagon Papers*, and the federal government investigates UUA bank records.

1974 Federal judge dismisses UUA Pentagon Papers Case without prejudice after US Attorney's statement that the investigation would not be resumed.

1979 Death of President Paul Carnes; election of President O. Eugene Pickett.

1983 Young Religious Unitarian Universalists (YRUU) succeeds Liberal Religious Youth (LRY).

1985 Election of President William F. Schulz.

$20,000,000 endowment given to the UUA by the North Shore Unitarian Universalist Society of Plandome, NY.

1987 Tabloid *Unitarian Universalist World* becomes *The World*, publishing in magazine format.

$9,000,000 grant for theological education given to UUA by the North Shore Unitarian Universalist Society of Plandome, NY.

1988 Emerson Professorship (in Unitarian Universalist studies) established at Harvard Divinity School.

1990 UUA delegation seeking guarantees of religious freedom enters Romania two weeks after the revolution.

Sister church program established between UUA and Transylvanian congregations.

1991 More than 400 ministers sign *New York Times* ad opposing Persian Gulf War.

1992 First meeting of the World Summit of Unitarian Leaders in Budapest, Hungary.

Beacon Press publishes bestselling book *The Measure of Our Success* by Marian Wright Edelman. Beacon author Mary Oliver wins National Book Award for poetry.

About the Unitarian Universalist Association

The Unitarian Universalist Association (UUA) represents the consolidation in 1961 of two religious denominations: the Universalists, organized in 1793 and incorporated in 1866, and the Unitarians, organized in 1825 and incorporated in 1847. The Association is composed of member congregations serving more than 200,000 adults and church school children in more than 1,000 churches and fellowships around the world.

The Association's policy-setting body is its General Assembly, which meets annually and is made up of delegates from the churches and fellowships. The General Assembly makes overall policy for carrying out the Association's purposes, reviews the program, and elects for stated terms a president, a moderator, a financial advisor, and four other members of the Board of Trustees. Twenty members of the Board are elected from districts. The Board conducts the affairs of the Association and carries out policies and directives as provided by law.

The churches and fellowships that constitute the Association's member bodies are completely autonomous and self-governing. Ultimate authority and responsibility is vested in the membership of each congregation. Membership is open to all without regard to color, race, sex, disability, affectional or sexual orientation, age, or national origin.

Continentally, the Association is organized into twenty-three geographic districts. Each district serves the congregations in its area with a variety of programs and promotes increased participation in the life of the denomination. Professional staff from the UUA and the districts offer counsel and assistance in many matters to districts, area councils or "clusters," and individual congregations.

Among the many functions and services of the Association are the following: aiding Unitarian Universalist (UU) congregations, organizing new groups, encouraging area leadership, providing building loans, producing pamphlets and devotional materials, keeping more than 100,000 UU families informed with issues of *The World* magazine, creating a sense of continental unity and purpose, maintaining interfaith relationships, providing financial advice, managing an investment trust, creating religious education curricula, exchanging information on social action, supporting a UU voice in Washington, accrediting men and women for the ministry, assisting congregations to find new ministers, and raising funds to accomplish and sustain the many programs of the Association. Beacon Press is a non-profit publisher dedicated to the responsible exploration of the human condition. Over half a million Beacon Press books are sold each year.

Many (but by no means all) Unitarian Universalist ministers receive their theological education at one of three schools: Meadville/Lombard Theological School, affiliated with the University of Chicago; Starr King School for the Ministry in Berkeley, CA; and Harvard (University) Divinity School in Cambridge, MA.

A number of organizations related to the Association address specific Unitarian Universalist needs. These include the UU Service Committee, the UU Women's Federation, the UU Ministers Association, Young Religious Unitarian Universalists, UU United Nations Office, and many others.

UU congregations in Canada have a national voice and conduct many programs through the Canadian Unitarian Council (Counseil Unitaire Canadien), with offices in Toronto.

The Association maintains contact with liberal religious groups throughout the world through the International Association for Religious Freedom, which has its headquarters in Oxford, England.

For further information on the Unitarian Universalist Association and related organizations, write to the UUA, 25 Beacon Street, Boston, MA 02108-2800. Or call us at (617) 742-2100.

About the Church of the Larger Fellowship

The Church of the Larger Fellowship (CLF) provides a ministry to isolated religious liberals who, for geographical or other reasons, are unable to attend a Unitarian Universalist congregation. CLF offers them a spiritual home within the Unitarian Universalist movement.

By mail, phone, and fax, CLF today serves a worldwide network of more than 2,200 members, including over 400 families with children and young people. CLF members live in some sixty-five countries, all fifty of the United States, and all the Canadian provinces. Women and men around the globe who cherish liberal religious convictions find a warm welcome, spiritual inspiration, personal pastoral support, religious education, and a variety of practical resources in this unique "church without walls."

CLF sends *Quest*, its monthly publication containing articles and sermons from UU perspectives as well as CLF and UU news, to each member. (*Quest* is also available on audiotape.) In addition, members receive the *World*, the bi-monthly magazine published by the Unitarian Universalist Association.

The church has its own full-time minister who is available to members for personal support and counseling, religious and theological discussions, and practical help. The minister's 24-hour, toll-free "800" line enables members to contact the minister directly as needed.

CLF maintains a small loan library of denominational resource materials adapted for home use. Library holdings include books on UU history and theology; Month of Sundays (sets of four complete worship services in large print); video- and audiotaped UU sermons; adult self-study courses; and religious education curricula for children and youth. The church's Director of Religious Education is available to consult with members about these resources and other religious education questions.

CLF also offers a program for small churches and fellowships that are experiencing a need for programming help and support, particularly with weekly worship and religious education programs for children. Called "Church-on-Loan," the program provides enrolled groups with professional guidance and access to a varied set of worship and religious tools from the CLF Loan Library resources.

The need for a "church from a distance" emerged early in the history of the United States. In 1825 Thomas Jefferson wrote to Dr. Benjamin Waterhouse, "The population of my neighborhood is too slender and is too much divided into other sects to maintain any one preacher well. I must therefore be contented to be a Unitarian by myself." Later, in 1884, "The Post-Office Mission" was organized. CLF is the legal and logical successor carrying on this church-by-mail.

First organized in 1944 under the auspices of the American Unitarian Association, CLF was incorporated in 1970 as an autonomous organization. The church is managed by its own board of directors, which is elected by and responsible to CLF members. A "member canvass" is held each fall to meet the expense budget; members pledge according to their commitment and ability to contribute. Members are also asked to support the UUA's Annual Program Fund.

To assist in meeting expenses, an endowment fund honoring Frederick May Eliot, a leader in the UU movement, and Clinton Lee Scott, a founding minister, creates a perpetual foundation. In addition, CLF has a "Society of Sponsors"—

individuals, many of whom are members and/or ministers of existing churches and fellowships, who recognize the service that CLF provides to the movement and contribute toward its mission. Not only does CLF introduce liberal religion to hundreds of new people each year, but many new congregations emerge from a nucleus of CLF members.

For further information about the Church of the Larger Fellowship, write to CLF, Unitarian Universalist, 25 Beacon Street, Boston, MA 02108-2823. Or call us at (617) 742-2100.

Selected Bibliography

BOOKS

Many of these titles are available from the UUA Bookstore: 25 Beacon Street, Boston, MA 02108; telephone (617) 742-2100.

Biography

Bainton, Roland H. *Hunted Heretic*. Boston: Beacon Press, 1953. A biographical study of Michael Servetus, the most famous of the sixteenth-century anti-Trinitarians, who was burned at the stake in Geneva in 1553.

Blanchard, Paula. *Margaret Fuller: From Transcendentalism to Revolution*. New York: Addison-Wesley, 1987. Inspiring story of great writer and feminist.

Cassara, Ernest. *Hosea Ballou: The Challenge to Orthodoxy*. Lanham, MD: University Press of America, 1982. A study of the life and works of the great nineteenth-century Universalist.

Commager, Henry Steele. *Theodore Parker: Yankee Crusader*. Boston: Skinner House, 1982. A biography of the Unitarian reformer, preacher, and scholar whom Ralph Waldo Emerson called one of the three great men of the age.

Coté, Charlotte. *Olympia Brown: The Battle for Equality*. Racine, WI: Mother Courage, 1988. Powerful story of pioneering woman minister of Universalism.

Hitchings, Catherine. *Universalist and Unitarian Women Ministers*. Boston: Unitarian Universalist Historical Society, 1985. Includes the biographies of more than 150 deceased Universalist and Unitarian women ministers.

Howlett, Duncan. *No Greater Love: The James Reeb Story*. Boston: Skinner House, 1993.

Hunter, Edith F. *Sophia Lyon Fahs: A Biography*. Boston: Beacon Press, 1976.

Kring, Walter. *Henry Whitney Bellows*. Boston: Skinner House, 1979.

Lutz, Alma. *Susan B. Anthony*. Boston: Beacon Press, 1960.

Marshall, George N. *A. Powell Davies and His Times*. Boston: Skinner House, 1990.

Mendelsohn, Jack. *Channing: The Reluctant Radical*. Boston: Skinner House, 1979. A contemporary biography of William Ellery Channing, a major nineteenth-century Unitarian leader.

Richardson, Robert D., Jr. *Henry Thoreau: A Life of the Mind*. Berkeley: University of California Press, 1987.

Rusk, Ralph L. *The Life of Ralph Waldo Emerson*. New York: Charles Scribner's Sons, 1949.

Schwartz, A. Truman, and John G. McEvoy, eds. *Motion Toward Perfection: The Achievement of Joseph Priestley*. Boston: Skinner House, 1990.

Skinner, Charles R., and Alfred S. Cole. *Hell's Ramparts Fell*. Boston: Universalist Publishing House, 1941. A biography of John Murray, the founder of American Universalism.

Voss, Carl Herman. *Rabbi and Minister: The Friendship of Stephen S. Wise and John Haynes Holmes*. Buffalo: Prometheus Books, 1980.

Contemporary Statements

Adams, James Luther. *On Being Human Religiously*. Boston: Beacon Press, 1976.

Buehrens, John A., and F. Forrester Church. *Our Chosen Faith: An Introduction to Unitarian Universalism*. Boston: Beacon Press, 1989.

Marshall, George N. *Challenge of a Liberal Faith*. 3d ed. Boston: Skinner House, 1987. An affirmation of Unitarian Universalist values with a brief account of beliefs and history.

Mendelsohn, Jack. *Being Liberal in an Illiberal Age—Why I Am a Unitarian Universalist*. Boston: Beacon Press, 1985.

Schulz, William F. *Finding Time and Other Delicacies*. Boston: Skinner House, 1992.

History

Ahlstrom, Sydney E., and Jonathan S. Carey. *An American Reformation: A Documentary History of Unitarian Christianity*. Middletown, CT: Wesleyan University Press, 1985.

Ballou, Hosea. *A Treatise on Atonement*. Introduction by Ernest Cassara. Boston: Skinner House, 1986. First published in 1805, this is the major work of the great nineteenth-century Universalist theologian.

Barbour, Brian M., ed. *American Transcendentalism*. Notre Dame, IN: University of Notre Dame Press, 1973. An anthology of criticism.

Bartlett, Laile. *Bright Galaxy: Ten Years of Unitarian Fellowship*. Boston: Beacon Press, 1960.

Cassara, Ernest. *Universalism in America*. Boston: Skinner House, 1984. A historical documentary of Universalism's first two hundred years.

Crompton, Arnold. *Unitarianism on the Pacific Coast: The First Sixty Years*. Boston: Beacon Press, 1957.

DiFiglia, Ghanda. *Roots and Visions: The First Fifty Years of the Unitarian Universalist Service Committee*. Boston: Unitarian Universalsit Service Committee, 1990.

Hewett, Phillip. *Unitarianism in Canada*. Canadian Unitarian Council/Conseil Unitaire Canadien, 1967. The origin of individual Unitarian and Universalist Churches in Canada as well as the history of the Canadian Unitarian Council.

__________. *Unitarians in Canada.* Ontario: Fitzhenry and White Side, 1978. How the Unitarians have exerted a powerful influence on Canadian life for more than 150 years.

Howe, Charles. *The Larger Faith: A Short History of American Universalism.* Boston: Skinner House, 1993.

Howe, Daniel Walker. *The Unitarian Conscience.* 2d ed. Middleton, CT: Wesleyan University Press, 1987. A study of moral philosophy taught at Harvard and its influence on outstanding New England Unitarians from 1805 to 1861.

Hutchison, William R. *The Transcendentalist Ministers.* New Haven, CT: Yale University Press, 1959. A study of nineteenth-century Transcendentalist ministers and their ideas.

Lavan, Spencer. *Unitarians and India: A Study in Encounter and Response.* Boston: Skinner House, 1977.

Lyttle, Charles H. *Freedom Moves West: A History of the Western Unitarian Conference.* Boston: Beacon Press, 1952.

Miller, Perry, ed. *The Transcendentalists.* Cambridge, MA: Harvard University Press, 1950.

Miller, Russell E. *The Larger Hope: History of the Universalist Church in America.* 2 Vols. Boston: Unitarian Universalist Historical Society, 1979-1985.

Morrison-Reed, Mark D. *Black Pioneers in a White Denomination.* Boston: Beacon Press, 1984.

Parke, David. *The Historical and Religious Antecedents of the New Beacon Series in Religious Education*. Ann Arbor, MI: University Microfilms International, 1978.

__________. ed. *The Epic of Unitarianism*. Boston: Skinner House, 1980. Original writings on the history of liberal religion from the sixteenth to the twentieth century.

Patton, Kenneth. *A Religion for One World*. Boston: Beacon Press, 1976. Major statement by influential humanist.

Persons, Stow. *Free Religion: An American Faith*. New Haven, CT: Yale University Press, 1947. A study of the origin, development, and implications of the free religious movement which emerged from Unitarianism following the Civil War.

Robinson, David. *The Unitarians and the Universalists*. Westport, CT: Greenwood Press, 1985.

Robinson, Elmo Arnold. *American Universalism: Its Origins, Organization, and Heritage*. Jericho, NY: Exposition Press, 1970.

Scott, Clinton Lee. *The Universalist Church of America: A Short History*. Boston: Universalist Historical Society, 1957. An introductory essay on the history of American Universalism.

Wilbur, Earl Morse. *Socinianism and Its Antecedents*. Vol. 1 in *A History of Unitarianism*. Cambridge, MA: Harvard University Press, 1945.

__________. *In Transylvania, England, and America.* Vol. 2 in *A History of Unitarianism.* Cambridge, MA: Harvard University Press, 1952. A definitive work on the origins of Unitarianism.

__________.*Our Unitarian Heritage.* Boston: Beacon Press, 1956. An introduction to the history of Unitarianism from early Christianity through the first quarter of the twentieth century.

Williams, George Huntston. *American Universalism: A Bicentennial Historical Essay.* Boston: Skinner House, 1983. A study of the first 100 years of Universalism with special attention to its impact on American society.

Wintersteen, Prescott B. *Christology in American Unitarianism.* Boston: Unitarian Universalist Christian Fellowship, 1977.

Wright, Conrad. *The Beginnings of Unitarianism in America.* Boston: Beacon Press, 1955. Examines eighteenth-century religious liberals as a unified group in the social structure of New England from 1735 to 1805.

__________. *The Liberal Christians.* Boston: Skinner House, 1979. Six essays that look at American Unitarian history in relation to some of the dominant forces in American life.

__________. *Three Prophets of Religious Liberalism: Channing, Emerson, Parker.* 2d ed. Boston: Skinner House, 1986. In addition to an introductory essay, includes William Ellery Channing's *Unitarian Christianity,* Ralph Waldo Emerson's *Divinity School Address,* and Theodore Parker's *The Transient and Permanent in Christianity.*

__________. ed. *A Stream of Light: A Sesquicentennial History of American Unitarianism*. Boston: Skinner House, 1975.

__________. *Walking Together: Polity and Participation in Unitarian Universalist Churches*. Boston: Skinner House, 1989.

Religious Education

Anastos, M. Elizabeth, and David Marshak. *Philosophy Making for Unitarian Universalist Religious Growth and Learning: A Process Guide*. Boston: Unitarian Universalist Association, 1983.

Anastos, M. Elizabeth, ed. *Curriculum Mapping: A Guide to Curriculum Planning for Unitarian Universalist Societies*. Boston: Unitarian Universalist Association, 1990.

Boys, Mary. *Educating in Faith*. San Francisco: Harper & Row, 1989.

Fahs, Sophia Lyon. *Today's Children and Yesterday's Heritage*. Boston: Beacon Press, 1952.

Holleroth, Hugo. *Relating to Our World*. Boston: Unitarian Universalist Association, 1974.

Johnson-Fay, Ellen, *et al.*, eds. *Unitarian Universalism in the Home*. Boston: Unitarian Universalist Association, 1982.

MacLean, Angus. *The Wind in Both Ears*. 2d ed. Boston: Skinner House, 1987.

Rosen, Harold. *Religious Education and Our Ultimate Commitment*. Lanham, MD: University Press of America, 1985.

Social Justice

Gilbert, Richard S. *The Prophetic Imperative.* Boston: Unitarian Universalist Association, 1980.

Unitarian Universalist Association. *Resolutions and Resources.* Boston: Unitarian Universalist Association, 1988. A Social Responsibility Handbook.

____________. *Task Force on Social Responsibility and Accompanying Paper #1*. Boston: Unitarian Universalist Association, 1985.

PERIODICALS

For subscription to periodicals, write directly to these addresses.

The Inquirer
"The oldest dissenting weekly paper in Britain," containing Unitarian news of England and the Commonwealth, plus articles of general interest. Essex Hall, 1-6 Essex Street, Strand, London, WC2R 3HY.

Proceedings of the Unitarian Universalist Historical Society
Research articles and critical reviews of current literature on the history of Unitarian Universalism. 25 Beacon Street, Boston, MA 02108-2800.

Religious Humanism
The quarterly journal of the Fellowship of Religious Humanists. P.O. Box 597396, Chicago, IL 60659-7396.

Synapse
The newspaper of the Young Religious Unitarian Universalists. Published several times per year. YRUU, 25 Beacon Street, Boston, MA 02108-2800.

Unitarian Universalist Christian
News, articles and sermons of Unitarian Universalist Christianity in the modern world. P.O. Box 66, Lancaster, MA 01523-0066.

World
The official journal of the Unitarian Universalist Association. 25 Beacon Street, Boston, MA 02108-2800.

PAMPHLETS

Contact the UUA Bookstore to inquire about the availability of these and other pamphlets.

General

Becoming a Member
Brief History of Unitarian Universalism
Come Join with Us
The Faith of a Humanist
The Faith of a Liberal Christian
The Faithfulness of Unitarian Universalists
The Five Smooth Stones of Liberalism
An Invitation to Growth
Journeys: The Many Paths to Unitarian Universalism
Meet the Unitarian Universalists
Spirituality: Unitarian Universalist Experiences

We Are
Welcome to Unitarian Universalism: A Community of Truth, Service, Holiness and Love

Life Issues

All Our Losses
Celebrating Birth, Marriage, Death, and Other Occasions

Religious Education

Can I Believe Anything I Want?
It's a New Day for Religious Education
Who Are the Unitarian Universalists?
Young Religious Unitarian Universalists

Social Justice

Facts on Military Service and Conscientious Objection
IARF: World Community of Religions for Service and Peace

"UUs Speak" Series

William Ellery Channing Speaks
Ralph Waldo Emerson Speaks
Sophia Lyon Fahs Speaks
Clarence Russell Skinner Speaks

"UU Views" Series

UU Views of the Bible
UU Views of Church
UU Views of Death and Immortality
UU Views of God

UU Views of Jesus
UU Views of Science and Religion

ADDITIONAL RESOURCES

Other materials are available from these sources.

Unitarian Universalist Service Committee, 130 Prospect Street, Cambridge, MA 02139-1813.

Unitarian Universalist United Nations Office, 777 UN Plaza, Suite 7D, New York, NY 10017.

Unitarian Universalist Women's Federation, 25 Beacon Street, Boston, MA 02108-2800.

A large and varied stock of books, pamphlets, and teacher resources relating to Unitarian Universalism are listed in the UUA Bookstore Catalog. For a free copy, call or write the UUA Bookstore, 25 Beacon Street, Boston, MA 02108-2800, (617) 742-2100.